WRITE & SELL A WELL-SEASONED ROMANCE

WRITE & SELL A WELL-SEASONED ROMANCE

LAUNCH YOUR AUTHOR JOURNEY IN LATE-LIFE ROMANCE

STELLA FOSSE

Copyright © 2024 by Stella Fosse.

All rights reserved. No portion of this book, except for brief review, may be reproduced, stored in a retrieval system, or transmitted in any form or by any means—electronic, mechanical, photocopying, recording, or otherwise—without the written permission of the publisher. For information contact the publisher.

ISBN: 978-1-950227-14-3

Cover by Diana Rosinus (www.dianarosinus.com/)

Published by:

Baubo Books

125 S Estes Drive #4311,

Chapel Hill, NC 27514, USA

www.stellafosse.com

ALSO BY STELLA FOSSE

Vampires of a Certain Age

[https://books.stellafosse.com/m8itcxkta0]

Brilliant Charming Bastard

[https://books.stellafosse.com/lxhhm0146s]

The Erotic Pandemic Collection

[https://books.stellafosse.com/lwnnhka5hm]

Aphrodite's Pen:
The Power of Writing Erotica After Midlife

[https://books.stellafosse.com/8m3bi2ibu3]

PREFACE

As you use this book to write your Well-Seasoned Romance, I ask you to practice through a series of exercises. Some of the exercises include forms that you should complete.

Of course, that doesn't work very well in an eBook, and even in the print edition the forms are small. To help you with this challenge, I have created a download pack that contains all the forms at full US Letter size for you to print. The pack also includes some examples from the book, such as a press release.

I'll remind you about the downloadable forms at various points in the exercises. To download them, submit your email address here: https://stellafosse.com/wsrdownload. The complete pack will arrive in your email box.

I'd love your feedback on what worked and what could be improved with the download pack. Please email your comments to stella@stcllafosse.com.

Many thanks, and enjoy your writing!
    Stella

CONTENTS

Introduction	xi
Part One: Write Your Well-Seasoned Romance	1
1. Ten Keys to Joyful Writing	3
2. What Makes a Romance a Genre Romance	17
(and a Seasoned Romance a Seasoned Romance)	
3. Build Your Premise	31
4. Create Your Main Characters	39
5. Create Sidekick Characters	53
6. Build the Romance Plot	61
7. Build the External Plot for Your Romance Novel	71
8. Act One — When Worlds Collide	77
9. Act Two Part One — The Conflict Builds	87
10. Act Two Part Two — The Big Breakup	95
11. Act Three — The Happy Ending	107
Part One: Conclusion & Resources	123
Part Two: Edit Your Well-Seasoned Romance	127
12. Editing Overview	129
13. The Cocoon Phase	131
14. Developmental Editing	133
15. Line Editing	139
16. Proofreading	145
Part Two: Conclusion & Resources	149
Part Three: Publish Your Well-Seasoned Romance	151
17. Publishing Overview	153
18. Traditional Publishing — With or Without an Agent	165
19. Hybrid Publishing	187
20. Indie Publishing	193
Part Three: Conclusion & Resources	201
Part Four: Sell Your Well-Seasoned Romance	205
21. Overview of Publicity and Marketing	207
22. Publicize Your Book	213
23. Market Your Well-Seasoned Romance	227

Part Four: Conclusion & Resources	239
Glossary of Terms and Abbreviations	243
About the Author	253
Stella Would Love To Know You Better!	255
Please Review This Book	257
Acknowledgments	259

INTRODUCTION

Why (and How) to Write and Publish Seasoned Romance

This book is for you, whether you've written ten books or zero, whether you are a Romance fan or a Romance skeptic, whether you are thirty or eighty. It's a soup-to-nuts guide to write, publish, and market a Romance novel with vivid older characters. But before we get to *how* to do it, let's talk about…

Why You Should Write Seasoned Romance

Back in the day, I could not wait to retire from my technical writing career to write every sexy, vibrant story I had in my head. Then I read an article in the *New York Times* Book Review section by a Romance writer in her fifties giving advice to her sister writers. Her message in a nutshell:

If you want to get published, create characters in their twenties.

Was the publishing industry that ageist? Had the demands of career and parenting made me miss the boat? No way would I let that happen. Right then and there I decided to push back by writing sexy characters my own age.

INTRODUCTION

The good news is that traditional publishers have been through a sea change in recent years. Indie publishing is eating their lunch, partly because more diverse voices are represented—including the voices of older women. Meanwhile the number of people over sixty keeps growing, and older women read a lot. We make up almost half of the enormous market for Romance novels. And many of us want to read about the love lives of people our age, not our children's ages. Look at reader reviews for Romance novels with older main characters and you will see comments like these:

> "There are not enough books with mature characters; therefore, I jumped on this one."
>
> "Being a woman who is now a part of the senior population, I deeply appreciate reading books with characters who live with the same hopes and dreams."
>
> "Reading the word 'menopause' in a Romance novel is rewarding."
>
> "Being a tad over 60 I enjoy reading books of Romance with more senior couples. With vibrant personalities."
>
> "I needed the reminder that love can happen at any time."

There are a lot of books out there, but not enough for this niche market. Recognizing that pent-up demand, more publishers are following the money and setting aside their biases. "Seasoned Romance" is the publishing sub-genre for Romance novels with main characters over forty—or even thirty. But *thirty?* That's lightly seasoned. Let's write characters in their fifties, sixties, and beyond, and call our books "Well-Seasoned Romance."

INTRODUCTION

The benefits of Well-Seasoned Romance start long before publication. First off, writing one of these novels is a great way to push back on our own internal ageism. You and I were steeped in gendered ageism long before we had the critical awareness to challenge it. That was the soup we swam in; the cartoons of our youth were packed with stereotypes. Think back to Sleeping Beauty and Maleficent: the former a young and beautiful (and entirely passive) "good" character, the latter an intriguing, assertive, older, "bad" character. Consider Snow White and the Wicked Witch, or Cinderella and the Evil Stepmother, or more recently the Little Mermaid and Ursula.

And media misrepresentation of older women continues. Reports from the Geena Davis Institute confirm that older women have few roles in television and movies, and when we do appear, we are typically depicted as foolish, decrepit, or dying. Granted, the social narrative is changing, but it's not changing fast enough.

Think about the women you know over fifty and the vivid lives they lead. Think about the new energy many of us find for creative passions as the demands of career and child rearing recede. Writing about such characters can give you a new perspective on your life, and that alone is reason enough to start writing.

The first person to whom a writer tells a story is herself. We empower ourselves by writing stories in which we portray powerful and interesting older people—rather like the people we know (and the people we are). Writing can be an important way to heal from the wounds the culture inflicted for decades. Better yet, as we develop positive attitudes about aging, the research shows we add years of health to our lives. Then, if you choose to share your story in writing groups and through publication, you will also push back on the ageism around us.

Bottom line: If we want older women to be seen as the vibrant people we are, then *we* have to make that happen.

INTRODUCTION

How to Write, Publish and Market Seasoned Romance

Enough about *why* we should write Seasoned Romance. Let's talk about *how* to do it. That's where this book comes in.

The book in your hands takes you step by step through the process, starting with highlighting joyful approaches to writing (and why that benefits you), then grounding you in the Romance genre, and continuing through creating Romance plot and characters, and finally developing a full story. Then we'll talk about editing, publishing and marketing your novel.

Throughout the book I use examples from my own Well-Seasoned Romance, *Vampires of a Certain Age*, to illustrate the stages of creation. A get-acquainted summary is below.

An Elevator Pitch* for *Vampires of a Certain Age*

> *The vampire Marion Chase runs a Chicagoland blood bank that is due for a routine FDA inspection. Marion is determined the inspectors will not find out that her company provides ethically sourced blood to vampires all over the Midwest. While lead inspector Rachel Sutter is increasingly attracted to Chase, her protégé, Luke Castleton, unearths some disturbing facts—even as he is falling for Amber, Marion's second-in-command.*

I organized this book to make the most of your writing and publishing experience. Part One covers writing. Each chapter focuses on a different stage in the Romance novel, from the initial meeting of your characters all the way to the happy ending. The chapters also coach you on the craft of writing, including setting, plot, characters, how to create dialogue that moves the story forward, and how to build a great love scene. Each chapter also includes writing prompts to take your writing in fun directions that build toward your full novel.

---

* You will learn how to write pitches (and loglines and taglines) in later chapters.

As you read, look for these vital concepts throughout the book. Keep them in mind as you create your story.

Vital Concepts in Writing Seasoned Romance

- **Write what you know** — and by now you know a lot. Harvest your experience of people, places, situations, events, along with a hefty dose of imagination.
- **Mix it up**: Take a person you knew in your twenties, put them in a place where you lived in your thirties, with a challenge you faced in your fifties. Add a twist you read about in a newspaper or heard about from a friend.
- **Raise the stakes** means adding risk and reward. For instance you might bet five dollars; in a novel your character bets five thousand.
- **Add sensory details** to bring readers into the scene. Sometimes you want to tell about an event; most of the time you want to bring your reader into the experience through sight, sound, touch, aroma and taste.
- **Make it fun**. Let your characters appreciate the absurdity of life.
- **Entwine your protagonists**: Your main characters will bounce off each other throughout the story, as they chase and run away from romance.
- **Create intimacy**: A Romance novel is a slow-motion seduction that begins at your characters' first meeting. Your characters will take turns advancing and withdrawing right up to the happy ending.

When you complete the first draft of your Romance novel, throw yourself a party and take a break. Then consult Parts Two through Four that advise you how to edit, publish and market your story to propel it out into the world.

INTRODUCTION

A Word about How to Use this Book

If you are a *new writer* who has never written and published a novel, welcome! This guide was created with the novice author in mind. A fledgling writer who reads every chapter, studies every craft section and completes each exercise will be well equipped to write, publish and market a Well-Seasoned Romance novel.

On the other hand, if you are an *experienced author* who wishes to expand into Seasoned Romance, this guide is also for you! The materials about Romance expectations and organization will likely be most helpful. You may also benefit from some of the later materials specific to publishing and marketing in the Seasoned Romance sub-genre. Feel free to browse!

One Piece of Advice for Everyone
When you come to a writing exercise in this book, please complete it. Glancing at it and moving on won't do the trick. And just as important: write freely from your memory and imagination, no stopping and no editing. All of us harbor an Inner Critic whose goal is to protect us from criticism, but that inner voice can hamper our creative efforts. Ask your Inner Critic to step aside so that you can play with ideas. Invite her back when you arrive at the Editing section; she can be a big help then. Keep in mind that all writing, and much of editing, is play.

This is an *exciting time* to be a writer because our options for publishing have never been greater. And for those of us past midlife, it's also an *exciting time of life* to be a writer because we have the dreams and experiences of all our years to draw upon. I've had the distinct pleasure of leading classes for writers over 65 on how to

INTRODUCTION

write Well-Seasoned Romance and I've seen first-hand that our age cohort is well endowed with ideas and verve. It is a thrill to capture those concepts and more in this book so that others may benefit. Please connect with me at www.stellafosse.com to discover upcoming classes.

Stories are how humans understand reality, so the more vibrant stories we tell, the better for us all. I'm so glad to have you along on this creative journey. Keep the keys clicking and above all…

Enjoy!

Stella Fosse,
    North Carolina, 2024

PART ONE: WRITE YOUR WELL-SEASONED ROMANCE

CHAPTER 1
TEN KEYS TO JOYFUL WRITING

Shh! Don't tell….

All those tropes about tortured writers struggling to find the next word are clever ploys. They're designed to seduce the world into admiring us for doing what comes naturally. Sure, writing can be tough when you're staring at a blank screen, or later when you feel done with your project when it isn't done with you. But here's the great secret: Writing is play—wonderful, grownup play. That is especially true when writing a first draft. And writing your first draft is exactly what you are about to do.

Feel free to tell people what a tough job writing is. Get all the admiration and sympathy you can handle. Then come back to your computer and use these ten key ideas to make writing the first draft of your Well-Seasoned Romance a fun ride. You'll find lots of prompts to choose from throughout this book, ready to kick your brain in unexpected directions. Check out as many as you'd like.

Then come back to this chapter for a refresher anytime you need a bounce.

THE TEN KEYS

Even though Romance is a highly structured genre, it's essential to keep your sense of play alive. Here are some ways to do that.

Key #1: There is no such thing as a "Bad Romance."

Writing a "bad" first draft is a great goal. And believing that your bad first draft is OK is, paradoxically, the secret to writing your best stuff. Tell your Inner Critic how much you value them, and then kindly ask them to step aside while you write. Reassure them that they'll have a turn later, when it's time to proofread. That will free you up to play with words. Because **the first draft is your creative play space.**

Key #2: Save Everything You Write.

You never know what might come in handy. A story that wasn't worth finishing? It might have a great love scene that will be just what you need, next week or years from now.

Key #3: Your Story Does Not Need to Be Serious.

A lot of Romance novels are serious business, peppered with natural disasters and life-threatening illnesses. In my novel *Vampires of a Certain Age*, for example, one of the main characters develops a terminal illness. Bear in mind, though, that your Romance novel can be just for fun if you want (Hint: a terminal illness may not be terminal when your love interest is a vampire). Make your story whatever you would like. It's your book.

To gauge your interest in writing a light story, or just to exercise your free-writing muscles, try a fanciful premise from the exercise below.

WRITING EXERCISE: A RANDOM PREMISE

Write down a series of five numbers between 1 and 7, with no two of the same number.

Done? Good. Now:

Use your number series to choose one item from each column in the chart below, going from left to right.

For example, I chose the number series 4, 2, 5, 7, 6. That means I pick the 4th row for Character A, the 2nd row for Character A's Role, the fifth row for Plot Element, the 7th row for Character B, and the 6th row for Character B's Role. The sentence I got? "Isabel, who despised eating fruit, took no notice of George, a champion crossword puzzler."

STELLA FOSSE

ABSURD PREMISE GENERATOR:

Character A and their Reaction to Character B

Row #	Character A	Character A's Role	Plot Element	Character B	Character B's Role
1	Jocelyn,	a professional pig wrestler,	was secretly in love with	Chris,	who raised miniature opossums.
2	Waldo,	who despised eating fruit,	took an instant dislike to	Charlotte,	the lead singer in a prominent polka band.
3	Henry,	an off-key opera singer,	was slightly attracted to	Winifred,	a motorcycle buff.
4	Isabel,	a dedicated rock painter,	was disgusted by	Larry,	the mayor of Dinosaur, Colorado.
5	Terry,	who collected dust bunnies,	took no notice of	Rose,	who had just lost $1 in Small Claims Court.
6	Claire,	an avid stamp collector,	felt terribly superior to	Freddie,	a champion crossword puzzler.
7	Barry,	a former circus clown,	was quite amused by	George,	who sneezed a lot.

Got your premise? Great! Now write for ten minutes about the romance between these two characters. In what ways are they in conflict? In what ways are they drawn to each other? What would a happy ending look like for these two silly people?

Is this exercise too absurd? Fair enough; but come back here if you tire of the serious stuff.

A Note about "Character A" and "Character B".

Back in the day, the lead characters in a Romance were often referred to as "she" and "he." That's because the Romance genre was restricted to heterosexual (as well as thin, white, able-bodied and young) love. But as the genre has opened up to characters who represent marginalized groups, it makes sense to refer to the mains as A and B.

You could also develop a main character C, if you're ambitious enough to write about a threesome.

Key #4: You Get to Play with the Materials of Your Life.

All those decades tucked away in your cranium belong to you. You can write it just as you remember it. Or you can cut it up and make a collage out of the pieces and mix memories with bits of imagination.

Try some of these prompts to develop material for your Romance novel. If you're writing for a certain block of time each day, one of these makes a great warmup at the start of a writing session.

- **There are Places I Remember**: Write about a place that is no longer there.
- **The Life I Never Lived**: Look back at a key decision in your life. Imagine you had made a different choice. Now write about that other life.
- **Mix and Match**: Write for five minutes about a person who perplexed you in your forties. Write for five minutes about a place you loved in your twenties. Write for five minutes about a memorable event from your fifties. Now, what do you get if you put the three of them together? Write about that combination for ten minutes.

Key #5: Shake up your imagination.

A great way to politely sidestep your Inner Critic is to entertain them. Try one of these techniques:

- **Dance for ten minutes**, then write.
- **Read something you love for ten minutes**, then write as that piece inspires you.
- **Write first thing in the morning**, when you are not quite awake. Or better yet, keep a dream journal. Leave a small notebook and a pen by your bed and write about your dreams just as you awaken.
- **Smell something nice**, like vanilla or cologne. Then write.
- **Access a photo site** like Pixabay and view pictures of people the age of your characters. Choose one photo to write about.
- **Try ten minutes of attitude**: Set a timer to go off every two minutes and switch attitudes in your writing each time the bell sounds. Start with rebellious; then grateful; fearful; proud; and finally, amused.
- **Write to instrumental music.** Try different styles and see what works best: Quiet classical? Bombastic symphonies? Cool jazz?
- **Pick a sentence at random from your favorite book**. Write it down and keep going. If you run out of steam, pick a different sentence and go again.

Key #6: Make it bigger.

The process of "raising the stakes" is a great technique in writing fiction, especially Romance.

Think back on a real life crisis from your thirties. How could you make the drama even bigger? If you lost your job, what if your former employer badmouthed you to potential employers? What if you lost your house too?

Next, remember something good that happened in your forties.

What if you make that even bigger? If you won a thousand dollars in the lottery, imagine you won a million.

Now write about both scenarios.

Key #7: Try NaNoWriMo.

Here's another way to convince your Inner Critic to step aside until it's time to proofread. Next October, sign up for National Novel Writing Month, a fun, free, online event which happens each November. You'll commit to write 50,000 words in a month. When you write that quickly, you'll leave your Inner Critic in the dust. NaNoWriMo also features lots of great, free resources for writers. And by the way, it's perfectly fine to outline your characters and plot in advance.

Key #8: Even editing can be fun.

Yes, you heard that right. More to come in a later chapter. For now, just be glad it's true.

Key #9: Everything you can imagine happened sometime and somewhere.

And you can write about whatever you want. You might imagine a time and place where fat older women are considered beautiful (Look up the Willendorf Goddess. There is nothing inevitable about our culture's fixation on youth and thinness).

Or imagine a world where older women scientists start a company that solves climate change (That's the premise of my first novel, *Brilliant Charming Bastard*).

And what about the choices you didn't make, the lives you never lived?

For the next ten minutes, write about a time and place *you* imagine.

Key #10: Structure can be freeing.

It's true. Writing a sonnet with a certain rhythm and a particular rhyming structure can pull your brain in unexpected directions. Having to work inside a frame can be a great stimulus to creativity, whether that frame is poetic form or a structured fictional form like Romance. That's what the next chapter is all about: What makes a "romance" a "Romance," and how Seasoned Romance messes with the original genre.

Onward! But first, if you are not already in a writing group, here are some ideas for how to start one.

WRITING CONCEPT: START A ROMANCE WRITING GROUP

Imagine meeting each month with a circle of older women as co-creators, joining together to celebrate our power and creativity. What could be more fun, and more liberating, than that? And there is no reason — absolutely none — why you and your friends (or friends-to-be) should not have that in your life.

When we explore Romance writing from our vantage point as older women, we draw on rich life experience. We look honestly at what we desire, and how our desires have played out through our lives. Writing solo is great, because we become visible to ourselves through writing. We learn what we want and who we are by seeing our reflection on the page. And we grow even more into our real selves by sharing our creations with our writing sisters. It could be just a couple of friends. You can begin with one friend, and each of you could invite another friend to join.

When Lynx Canon and I started a writing group years ago, we set up agreements that enabled each of us to feel safe sharing vulnerable writing. Everyone in the group agreed to provide only positive feedback on first drafts, and everyone had the right to pass without question when it was time to read our work aloud. We explored ways to entice the muse through writing prompts and structured writing. And for inspiration, we looked at the canon of sexy literature already written by older women. The result was a creative sisterhood that lives on years after its founding. That joyful experience of sharing our writing, that wild mystery we found in one another, is an opportunity that should be available to women writers everywhere.

Imagine if every town had a group like that. Imagine if, no matter where you lived, you could find a circle of writers who would laugh with you at the foibles of humanity and celebrate your untamed imagination. What a mutiny against the invisibility of older women. What a foundation to express our wisdom and power.

It all begins with you. Whisper "Romance novel" to your friends, and see which ones perk up their ears. They need not have written before—the key is to play, with no judgment, as a gateway to our creative selves. Share your writing with each other, praise what you like about it, and then explore character, plot, dialogue, in a spirit of playfulness.

The purpose of a writing group goes even beyond the support and inspiration we share among ourselves. There is a reason why human females live so long after our reproductive years: to share what we know with the younger ones. Society does a poor job of heeding us, but we can help to awaken it. So many women in our sixties and beyond find that this is the happiest time of our lives, and when we let younger women in on that secret, it's inspiring for them as well as for us. Our writing group had the opportunity to read in public for audiences that included younger adults, and we heard back from many of them about the relief they felt when they learned of the joy and creativity they too can find in the years ahead. Too often, popular culture leaves the mistaken impression that sensuality and romance end at some arbitrary birthday. By sharing and publishing our writing, we can enlighten younger adults and push back on the ageism that harms us all.

This could be the start of a fun revolution: a celebration of older women's vision and agency. Maggie Kuhn, a true mutineer and founder of the Gray Panthers, called for "Learning and sex until rigor mortis." Let's add Romance to the list.

WRITING CHALLENGE: A WEEK OF AGE-POSITIVE WRITING PROMPTS

Here is a set of prompts that will attune your mindset to write about love and lust after midlife. And while we are at it, writing from prompts like these could add to our health and longevity. We know that age positivity is good for us. Pushing back on internalized ageism helps us live longer, healthier, happier lives. We also know that creativity is powerfully important, especially during our older years. And, too, the tales we tell define our reality. As the poet Muriel Rukeyser wrote, "The universe is made of stories, not of atoms."

So here's the challenge: Write from a pro-age writing prompt every day for a week. But this is play, not work! Even though it's good for us, the number one reason to write is to **enjoy**.

What's that? You're not used to thinking of writing as fun? Here are ten rules to make it so.

Rules for this Seven Day Free Write:

- **There are no rules**. That includes: If you don't like the writing prompt, change it.
- **Everyone is a writer**. This means you. We spend our lives spinning stories about ourselves and the world around us, and then make choices based on our stories (Remember that "mistake" you made, years ago? How did it change your story?).
- **Set a timer for five minutes.** You'll be amazed how much you can write in that time.

- **Write the first thing that comes to mind** and just keep going. No edits, no cross outs. It's naptime for your Inner Critic—play them a lullaby.
- **If you get stuck, write the same word over and over** until the next word comes. Just keep going.
- **Be as outrageous as you possibly can**.
- **Love what you write while you write it**. Everybody has an Inner Cheerleader. Invite yours to the party.
- At the end of five minutes: You did it! Yay! **What you wrote is just for you.** Writing benefits the writer, first and foremost. If you want to share your free write, great, but you don't need to.
- **If you are thinking of editing** what you wrote, first **put your free write aside** for at least a week. That way you'll appreciate it more.
- And if you decide to share and publish your pro-age writing, brava you! **We can all be part of the fun revolution** and use our creativity to shift the culture.

Now the Fun Part… The Seven Daily Prompts

What we want is to be renegades. What we want is to turn every trope about women after midlife upside down.

Ready? Set your timer for five minutes and… Go!

Day One:
She wrote an Anti-Bucket List of everything she was no longer willing to do.

Day Two:
When I am an old woman, I shall dye my hair purple.

Day Three:
At fifty she had no lovers. At sixty she had three.

Day Four:
She walked into that room like the ancestors sent her.

Day Five:

"Women have a special corner of their hearts for sins they have never committed."

(Cornelia Otis Skinner)

Day Six:

"What is hidden and mysterious in the ordinary life... in this neighborhood of scars and desires."

(Rene Johns, in *Aphrodite's Pen: The Power of Writing Erotica after Midlife*)

Day Seven:

"I am out with lanterns, looking for myself."

(Emily Dickenson)

"Help! I Hate Today's Prompt."

Good for you! Be a true renegade: Write about something else. Make up your own prompt, or try one of these bonus extras:

- She'd had children as an excuse to buy toy dinosaurs. But now the children were grown. *(Does she invent a line of dinosaur sex toys?)*
- "It doesn't take much to be considered a difficult woman. That's why there are so many of us." (Jane Goodall)
- "I have a next life bucket list: More sex. Better singing voice. The ability to tan." (Billie Berlin, in *Aphrodite's Pen: The Power of Writing Erotica after Midlife*)
- "All discarded lovers should be given a second chance, but with somebody else." (Mae West)
- "Our sexuality is the material of life, and to deny it in old age is to deny life itself." (Maggie Kuhn, founder of the Gray Panthers)
- "The older one gets, the more one likes indecency." (Virginia Woolf)
- "You can only be young once, but you can be immature forever." (Dave Barry)

- Write your revenge—because anything can happen on the page (For ideas, see my novel *Brilliant Charming Bastard: Getting Rich is the Best Revenge*).
- Or try writing a limerick—here's an example:

> A vivid old lady named Ruth
> Said, "It's true, I am long in the tooth,
> So I dress for success,
> Which means wearing less,
> And focus on being uncouth."`

(See *Aphrodite's Pen* for more limerick ideas and examples.)

You can also create your own seven-day challenge based on these extra prompts.

And now the next chapter, and the serious stuff: Just what is the recipe for Romance?

CHAPTER 2
WHAT MAKES A ROMANCE A GENRE ROMANCE
(AND A SEASONED ROMANCE A SEASONED ROMANCE)

Many novels include a romance between two lead characters. Many even include a subplot with a second romance between two supporting characters. But only some of those novels fit the conventions of the Romance genre, and dedicated Romance readers know the difference.

> News flash: Just because a novel contains a romance does not mean it is a capital-R Romance. The Romance genre has very specific requirements—as does the Seasoned Romance sub-genre.

Let's start with a summary of what makes a "romance" a "Romance," given today's genre expectations.

Word Count Expectations for a Genre Romance

While most novels published today are in the 60,000 to 80,000 word range, Romance novels tend to be at the shorter end, with many at the 50,000 word count. In general, the high cost of paper is exerting downward pressure on word count. You won't see many 100,000 word novels being published these days!

Keep in mind, though, that many Romance readers love reading a series. So if your story includes interesting side characters, consider giving them their own separate novels down the line.

Plot Requirements of a Genre Romance
In most fiction, the main plot is driven by external events. There might be a war, or a plague, or dinosaurs escape their enclosure.

A Romance novel is different. **In a genre Romance, the main driver of the plot is the romance itself.** Sure, external things happen, but the main plot looks like this, every time:

- **Act One:** We are introduced to two (or three, if you're adventurous) good but flawed people who then meet and are drawn to one another. But their conflicts are made clear.
- **Act Two, Part One:** The main characters develop doubts about forming a relationship and alternate between getting closer and backing away. This part ends with a "false high" (It looks like the characters are starting a romance) or a "false low" (It looks like the characters will never get together). Neither scenario lasts.
- **Act Two, Part Two:** The dance of ambivalence intensifies, and by the end of this part, there is a huge betrayal of trust. It looks like the main characters are done with each other for good.
- **Act Three:** Now that they're firmly apart, the characters experience massive regret. They each come to terms with the inner wounds that drove them apart, and they are reunited in love (and, probably, sex). This part may end with an Epilogue, where we see the lovers later in their happy lives together.

As you can tell, character ambivalence drives the romance plot. Uncertainty is essential. The middle of the story will include many plot twists as characters take turns chasing and running away, driven by the interplay of their mutual attraction and their inner wounds. Eventually, though, they build trust in one another and love conquers all.

In former times, every genre Romance was required to have a Happily Ever After ending, preferably with a big wedding. These days a Happy For Now ending is acceptable too.

So that's the essence of the Romance plot. In later chapters we will deconstruct each phase in detail, but that in a nutshell is the storyline that drives every Romance novel. And that plot is incredibly satisfying for the readers who make this genre a perennial favorite.

ROMANCE PLOT EXAMPLE

To illustrate, here is a high-level summary of the plot from my Seasoned Romance novel, *Vampires of a Certain Age*.

- **Act One:** Rachel, an FDA inspector in her fifties, arrives at a blood bank run by Marion, a 500-year-old vampire. The two smart women and natural adversaries are attracted to one another.
- **Act Two, Part One:** During the inspection at her blood bank, Marion hides the fact that she is supplying ethically sourced blood to midwestern vampires. Despite their growing mutual attraction, Rachel does her job and keeps finding clues.
- **Act Two, Part Two:** Rachel unearths Marion's secret and realizes Marion has been lying to her, while Marion tries to resist the appeal of Rachel, the exact image of her long-dead love. Rachel believes Marion is selling infected blood and tries to have Marion arrested but instead, Rachel falls deathly ill.
- **Act Three:** Marion saves Rachel's life by changing her to a vampire. Rachel and Marion become lovers. Rachel now sees the benefit of Marion's hidden business. And Marion begins to realize there is much more to learn from the

biology of vampires. In the Epilogue, the women create a research institute to study vampire biology.

In later chapters we will delve deeply into Romance plot structure. And as you have likely gathered, planning your plot is important.

WRITING CONCEPT: "PANTSERS" VERSUS "PLANNERS"

Writers often describe themselves as Pantsers (those who write by the seat of their pants) or Planners (those who set up a detailed outline before writing word one). In reality, most of us fall somewhere in between. We might plan some books more than others, or plan characters but not plot.

Because a Romance novel exists within a tight set of expectations, it makes sense to plan the outline of your novel ahead of writing it. Making up the story as you go may be more your style but is less likely to lead to a novel you can legitimately claim is Romance.

Using the tools in the chapters ahead, you will build out your story outline and know where you're going—and be confident that your finished manuscript will fit the Romance genre.

Character Requirements of a Genre Romance

The requirements for Romance main characters (the ones who will enjoy the happy ending) are as follows:

- They each have interesting lives at the start of the story, before they meet one another
- They each have reservations about getting involved in a relationship—reservations that spring from something in each one's backstory, something that has left them with inner wounds or flaws

- They are both capable of acting out their ambivalence by reaching out and then running away in various permutations
- And they both are capable of self-reflection, change, and ultimately building a trusting relationship.

Most non-Romance novels have a protagonist (a good guy) and an antagonist (a bad guy). In Romance, the two main characters are both protagonists **and** they are both antagonists. Sorting out their character conflicts resolves the plot.

Beyond the main characters in a genre Romance are the **sidekick characters**. Each main character typically has a confidante, a person who knows their backstory (their personal history) and gives the main characters feedback about their new relationship. The sidekick characters let us in on the main character's backgrounds and motivations when it suits the purposes of the author.

These requirements for plot and character are the heart of the Romance structure. In my novel, *Vampires of a Certain Age,* one of the main characters is several centuries old. In her mortal life, Marion Chase was a medieval herbal healer. Here is a description of her from early in the story, just after she becomes a vampire.

> On the night the men invaded her clearing, torches in hand, Marion Chase was nearing forty years old—longer than the lifespan of most women of that time. She wore long skirts and a laced-up bodice in the custom of the day. Her hair was wavy and black, with lines of silver just beginning. Her hands were stained green and brown from her work with concoctions. Strong hands, a woman's hands. But her strength had limits, until now. As their horse walked under a tree with a thick, low-hanging branch, Marion, unthinking, broke off the branch with one hand and wondered at her new strength.

By the present day, when Marion is a blood bank president, her physical appearance is basically unchanged (meaning she appears to be in her fifties, because Marion had already lived longer than the medieval lifespan when she became immortal). But her outlook has been shaped by five centuries of experience. She is in command now, and somewhat bemused by her new sidekick, Amber, who gives Marion a reason to begin adding backstory to the narrative. The scene where Marion and her sidekick meet is included at the end of this chapter.

Some people call Romance "formulaic," but then a sonnet is also highly structured, and nobody calls a sonnet "formulaic." On the contrary: When it comes to sonnets, the view of many literary critics is that the structure of a sonnet spurs creativity within the form.

Most sonnets deal with love, just as Romance novels do, but sonnets are even more tightly controlled. The rhythm, the number of syllables in each line, the pattern of rhymes, all are prescribed. And yet there is great variation in their content and style. To illustrate that concept of variation within a form, here are excerpts from two well-known examples of Victorian sonnets. The first is a meditation on love and death.

Remember
    By Christina Rossetti

> *Remember me when I am gone away,*
> *Gone far away into the silent land;*
> *When you can no more hold me by the hand,*
> *Nor I half turn to go yet turning stay.*

The second is just the opposite: a celebration of the expansiveness of love.

Sonnets from the Portuguese #43: How Do I Love Thee?
    By Elizabeth Barrett Browning

> *How do I love thee? Let me count the ways.*
> *I love thee to the depth and breadth and height*
> *My soul can reach, when feeling out of sight*
> *For the ends of being and ideal grace.*

These are such different poems, with different modes of expression and different meaning, even though each poet's word choices were circumscribed by the sonnet form. In the same way, the Romance plot circumscribes your choices as a writer. But the Romance form also frees you to design something wild and outrageous within that predefined structure. Your novel will be unique in the same way that each of Rossetti's and Browning's sonnets are unique.

Romance has lots of room for creativity, especially now, as publishers seek out Romance novels about people of color, queer people, and people with disabilities. And there is "Seasoned

Romance," a designation publishers give to tales about characters in midlife and beyond.

WRITING CONCEPT: THE CHECKERED HISTORY OF THE ROMANCE NOVEL

Writers after midlife are well qualified to write Romance. We have been there and done that. Yet in the past, one of the genre expectations for Romance was that the main characters would be young. Fortunately the scope of Romance characters has broadened. With the advent of the Seasoned Romance sub-genre, those of us who have enjoyed long lives can bring our experience to bear. We can create vibrant characters that reflect our lives and the lives of people we know.

These recent changes to the genre are only the latest iteration in the long history of the genre. The Romance genre did not always look like it does today—or like it did fifty years ago. The development of the genre has its own convoluted plot—and the story is not over yet.

Origins of the Romance Novel

In the early twentieth century, novels for women provided messages of refinement. Publishers were reluctant to run afoul of purity associations run by prominent men of the time. But then the first "best-sellers" arose: so-called "sex novels" that focused on women's sexual desires and pleasures. The success of books like May Sinclair's *The Helpmeet* (1907) and Victoria Cross' *The Greater Law* (1914) drove the expansion of the publishing industry. The most notorious novel of that era, *Three Weeks* by Elinor Glyn, told the story of a married woman's brief affair with a young Englishman.

These books paved the way for the Romance novels of the 1920s, including *The Well of Loneliness* by Radclyffe Hall. This was the first successful novel to portray a relationship between two women. Originally published in England, the book was tried for obscenity in

1928 and the court ordered all copies destroyed. Although efforts to censor this book in the United States were unsuccessful, *Well* was not republished in England until 1949.

From the beginning, critics have disdained Romance novels, especially those written by women. And yet these books explored women's desire and its attendant issues in ways that other writing did not. As a result, Romance continues to be the best selling genre in fiction.

Recent History of the Genre

In the 1950s and 1960s, Romance expanded to include career women such as stewardesses, and many novels were set in exotic locations. Then in 1972, a new category of "bodice rippers" began with the publication of *The Flame and the Flower* by Kathleen Woodiwiss, which sold over two million copies. The independent yet virginal heroines of bodice rippers were dominated by alpha male characters. Novels of this type often included sex scenes that we would now consider rape. By now the bodice ripper is a relic of the past, but these novels were extremely popular for many years.

Some of the best known Romance authors began their careers around this time, including Jackie Collins, Nora Roberts and Danielle Steel. In the Romance novels of the later twentieth century, the defining features were the preeminence of the romantic plot and the Happily Ever After ending (typically with a big wedding).

Beverly Jenkins, an African American author, has written Romance novels since the 1990s. But until recently, Jenkins was an exception in a genre that focused on white characters.

Romance Novels Today

In the Romance novels of the twenty-first century, romance and a happy ending remain the defining features. Romance is the driver, and the external plot remains secondary. The genre continues to be based on a standard three act structure with characters drawn to each other yet ambivalent. The main characters don't get together until they overcome their character flaws and reservations, allowing them to develop trust. All this is well established. However, the genre has evolved in several key ways.

First, the ending can now be Happy For Now rather than Happily Ever After. Maybe the characters marry and maybe they do not. Love takes many forms.

And while Romance was traditionally woman-meets-man, these days a Romance can also be woman-meets-woman, man-meets-man, person-meets-person, or even three-people-meet. A prominent example of queer Romance is *Red, White, and Royal Blue*. This 2019 novel by Casey McQuiston won the Goodreads Choice Awards for Best Romance and Best Debut Novel that year.

There is more racial diversity among Romance writers and characters than before. For example, Georgia political icon Stacey Abrams has written eight Romance novels under the pen name Selena Montgomery. And Julia Quinn's *Bridgerton* novels have been produced on Netflix by Shonda Rhimes with great success.

Plus size representation in Romance is also expanding, reminding us that stories of fat characters are worthy of being told. *Too Much Temptation* by Lori Foster was one of the first when it was published in 2007.

Areas for growth remain. While several recent Romance novels feature characters with disabilities, often the plot involves an able-bodied character "saving" a character with a disability (for example, a physical therapist falls in love with a recently disabled patient and teaches him about his own disability). Romance novels that center the voices of people with disabilities will be a welcome addition to the Romance genre.

Along with other forms of diversity, the rise of the Seasoned Romance has accompanied the rise in the number of readers over fifty and sixty. When Nan Reinhardt's agent pitched her first novel in 2019, editors at several publishing houses asked the writer to knock two decades off the ages of her main characters. Reinhardt refused.

Once More from the Top became a best seller and the first in her popular series, "The Women of Willow Bay."

Next Up: The Highly Seasoned Romance

The cohort of women in our fifties, sixties and beyond continues to grow. And as our numbers grow, so does awareness of the lack of representation of our vivid lives. Author Lynne Spreen switched to writing Romance because, as she put it, "I want to read about people my age, or at least over fifty. The wide-eyed newby isn't as compelling to me as the woman or man who has been kicked around a bit. Who has suffered, learned, and grown." And though there are more Romance novels with characters over fifty, barriers remain. Writer Sandra Antonelli points to bias in the publishing industry. One editor even said to her, "No one wants to read *granny sex*."

Antonelli, who wrote her graduate thesis on older women in fiction, sees Seasoned Romance as a way for women to reinforce more accurate perceptions of women over fifty as vibrant, inherently sexy people. She points out that these depictions are valuable for young women, too, as a way to envision a positive future.

One goal in this book is to connect the craft of writing with your experience creating Well-Seasoned Romance. In future chapters you will see craft sessions on dialogue, scene-building, and more. Later chapters will explore marketing craft as well. Here is the first Writing Craft section on autofiction, which is part autobiography and part fiction.

WRITING CRAFT: AUTOFICTION

All fiction draws at least partly on our life experience. But in autofiction, you become intentional about mixing and matching material from your past with something extra that you imagine. You might write about a friend or lover from long ago, put them into a situation you experienced in another part of your life, in a place you recall from yet another era in the past.

Autofiction is a great tool for Writers of a Certain Age because we have long, rich lives to draw upon. We have varied experiences of people, places and events to combine in fascinating ways. And autofiction gives us the freedom to create new stories with the grit and passion of memory plus the new directions where those combined memories take our imaginations.

AUTOFICTION AS MIX-AND-MATCH

Imagine writing about your life, making great use of the knowledge you have in a situation, yet adding details from your imagination that transform the story into something new. The result will be a story that captures the minds of your readers with the vividness of both real life and story.

Imagine matching an old friend's best qualities with the character flaws of someone else in your history. Imagine the main character in your story as yourself but living the life of a relative you knew well—or an ancestor you never met. Imagine setting the story in a place or time you remember vividly, even if it no longer exists.

The combinations in autofiction are endless and great fun to explore.

WRITING EXERCISE: AUTOFICTION QUICK WRITE

Think back on a crush from your past who did not reciprocate your interest.

- What obstacles might have arisen had you and that person actually dated?
- How might those obstacles have been resolved?
- And then—what kind of happy ending can you imagine?

Place the action in a different location from your past.
Write for ten minutes about "The One Who Got Away."

Each scene in your novel should have at least one purpose, which may include introducing or developing a conflict, or revealing key information about a character. The scene below explores the relationship between a main character and her sidekick, while enlisting the reader's curiosity about the main character's history, or backstory.

SCENE FROM *VAMPIRES OF A CERTAIN AGE*

There were days when Marion longed for the sixteenth century, witch trials and open sewers notwithstanding. But here she was, trapped in the age of fast food, as her new employee Amber Pettis unwrapped a cheeseburger. The scent of carrion wafted across her desk.

"Sorry to eat in your office, Marion. Noon was the only time we could meet. Here," Amber waved a French fry. "I have lots. Want some?"

Marion shook her head. "No, thank you. I'm not hungry."

"Are you ever?"

Marion arched one eyebrow. "I beg your pardon."

"Seriously, I have never seen you take one bite of food." Amber lifted the sandwich to her mouth. The dripping catsup was a nice deep red. The rest of the meal looked fake, like paper mâché food.

Amber chewed with gusto, then swallowed. "Are you on some diet?"

"You could say that."

"How long have you been on it?"

"About five hundred years."

Amber giggled and covered her mouth with her napkin. "I'll bet it feels like that."

"It does." Marion toyed with telling Amber who she really was, a mistake she made with a mortal every century or so. Although the fact that her blood bank did not have a single window might have been a clue.

"So... what do you eat?"

"It's a liquid diet, really."

Amber laughed. "Remember when people used to say, 'I'm on a liquid diet,' and meant they only drank booze?" She stopped laughing. "You're not an alcoholic, are you?"

"Not even close."

"Well then, what?" Amber paused. With any luck she had just remembered she was talking with the blood bank president. But Amber continued undaunted.

"Oh—am I being insensitive? Is it a medical condition?"

"Yes, it is medical, actually. I don't mind you asking. But if I explained you might be offended."

"Is it a religious thing? Because, you know, I'm not religious. But I don't mind if other people are."

Marion smiled. "In a way. I am sure I believe in things that you don't."

CHAPTER 3
BUILD YOUR PREMISE

The **premise** is the foundation of your tale. It is the one-line answer to the question: *What is your story about?* And in a Romance, of course, the premise centers on the main characters.

Not that the premise tells the whole story; far from it. Two writers could start with the same concept and come up with totally different results. What the premise ***does*** do is give you a starting point from which to tell the story to yourself. Because, after all, you are your first (and most important) reader.

Conventional Romance Tropes

The Romance genre depends on a few stock tropes: themes that appear in many published novels. Some of the standard tropes practically scream twenty-something.

- **Accidental Pregnancy**: *A one-night stand leads to a baby—and love.* Not happening in *my* books.
- **Forced Proximity:** *Stuck in an elevator, on a desert island, etc.* I find this concept less appealing than I would have thirty years ago, but if you like it, go for it.

- **Fake Relationship:** *Pretending to be interested for some social reason, then falling in love.* We're past that nonsense—aren't we?
- **Marriage of Convenience**: *Often used in historical novels.* Thank goodness, we are unlikely to face such pressures in this era, and at this stage of life.
- **Royalty, Sheikhs, Celebrities and Billionaires**: Meh. Probably not.
- **Workplace Romance**: By now, we know better than to date where we work. Or at least we should….
- **Runaway Brides**: Spare me.

But other standard tropes are natural concepts for Seasoned Romance:

- **Enemies-to-Lovers:** Two adversaries fall in love (as in *Vampires of a Certain Age*, where an FDA inspector falls in love with the president of a company she is inspecting).
- **Friends-to-Lovers:** Old friends suddenly see one another differently. For example, if two couples have been friends for decades, in later years the surviving spouse from each couple might console each other. This could be two widows surprised to find they are bisexual after a lifetime living as straight (as in one of the stories in my *Erotic Pandemic Collection*).
- **Second Chance Romance:** After a long break, former lovers find one another. These days we hear a lot about high school sweethearts reconnecting on social media half a century later. This is a great premise for a late-life Romance with a built-in conflict: *Why did they break up in the first place?*

A premise can start with any situation that is realistic for an older person. For instance, a Romance novel could involve two main characters who are widowed and reluctant to become involved again, or characters who are mutually attracted but their children wish to "protect" them from heartbreak. But you may decide to be even bolder. When you choose the premise for your story, you can refuse to be constrained by social conventions. Start with a what-if question that pushes boundaries. Remember that the first draft of your novel is your playground. No one gets to judge it or tell you what not to write —not even your own Inner Critic.

The Counter-Trope Premise

One way to access that brave place is to use a Counter-Trope: A premise that flies in the face of what is expected of older people, including olders of color, or queer, disabled, or fat older people. My Romance novel, *Vampires of a Certain Age*, is an Enemies-to-Lovers Romance that plays with the premise that even a 500-year-old woman is not too old for sex.

After 500 years, Marion Chase was surely immune to falling in love. And by now she was certain that no FDA inspector would ever figure out that Marion's blood bank fed most midwestern vampires. Then Rachel Sutter walked in the door, clipboard in hand, and proved Marion wrong on both counts.

Here are some examples of concepts based on counter-tropes that push the envelope for Seasoned Romance.

WRITING CONCEPT: COUNTER-TROPES

EACH OF THESE STORYLINES FLIPS THE DOMINANT SOCIAL NARRATIVE ABOUT OLDER PERSONS.

- A 50-year-old man falls in love with a 65-year-old career woman who is too busy to date him.
- A 55-year-old woman has three lovers and decides to get serious with just one of them. How to break it to the others? And what happens next?
- A woman who has always ignored her appearance inherits money at sixty and on a whim decides to get a makeover. With a new look from head to toe, she becomes a late life style icon—but how to know whether the woman who interests her cares about her for who she is, or for her looks? Or, worse yet, for her money?
- A 70-year-old dominatrix meets a 60-year-old dominant man, setting off a power struggle of epic proportions.
- Two people in their sixties go on one date at the start of the pandemic and choose to lock down together for sex (I test drove this premise in *The Erotic Pandemic Collection*).
- The Late Bloomer Trope: A woman who has never been interested in romantic love discovers sex in her fifties. The person who falls in love with her has a rough time persuading her to settle down.

WRITING EXERCISE:

Pick a premise from the Counter Trope list above and write for twenty minutes, with no stopping and no editing.

WRITING CRAFT: WRITING ABOUT SETTING

The premise and setting of a story are interdependent. Whether your character surfs, or sells emus, or climbs granite cliffs, some settings will work better than others. Providing sensory impressions of the setting, whether it's the smell of formaldehyde in a morgue or the sounds of rides at a state fair, gives the reader a sense of immediacy. In the passage below, Marion's fifteenth century stone cottage has a role in the plot and is presented to our senses as if it were a character.

Marion smelled the wolf and the wolf could smell her. He rattled the door against the latch, as she sat with her back against the rough oak to keep him out. And he, on the other side, snuffled through the gap between door and frame, with his ragged breath and his hunger. Her body was a better prize than the vermin in the woods, if only he could reach her.

In front of Marion a single candle burned on an oak table draped with mint and verbena and sage, materials of her trade. As the hours passed with the wolf still outside, Marion began to nod, so tired, and half-dreamed of feeding a deadly potion to the wolf; but no, he would eat her first.

The shutters were closed and barred for the night, so she could neither see nor hear what the wolf perceived across the clearing. She only knew that at some point in their grim visit, as she drifted in and out of exhausted sleep, the wolf grew distracted. The rough breath through the doorframe hesitated, stopped, and he was gone. But why?

In the exercise below, you are invited to play with premise and setting. For a downloadable copy you can fill in on your computer, please go to https://stellafosse.com/wsrdownload.

WRITING EXERCISE: THE PREMISE AND THE SETTING

Premise	Settings that Work
Character A is a last-minute substitution on a space mission. Character B is the captain and opposes the change.	
Character A is the ghost of Character B's long-lost love.	
Characters A and B went on a date at the start of lockdown and decided to shelter together.	
Character A is the penniless heir to a rundown English estate and marries a rich American, Character B, for their money.	
Character A is famous, and Character B is completely unimpressed.	
Character A laid off Character B years ago; now they are both retired.	
Character A is mourning the death of their spouse and tells Character B there can be no romance.	
Character A finds their high school sweetheart, Character B, online.	
Character A is widowed, and Character B has divorced three times.	
Character A jilted Character B long ago and sees now that it was a mistake.	
Character A is a developer and Character B is an environmentalist.	
Character A is the publicist for Character B, a writer whose books do not sell.	
Character A is terminally ill and marries a friend (Character B) so the friend will receive benefits—but then Character A recovers.	

Before we move on to the next chapter and create your main characters, let's try another approach to defining story elements: A random premise and setting generator.

Pick a series of four numbers from 1 to 7 (for example, you might choose 1-4-2-6). Then find your premise in the table below, with your first number determining your Character A, the second number determining your Character B, etc. For example, the series above, 1-4-2-6, yields: "A retired auto mechanic and a financial advisor discover they are estranged cousins while one of them is in the hospital."

ABSURD PREMISE AND SETTING GENERATOR

Use your four numbers to pick one box from each column

	Character A	Character B	Conflict	Setting
1	A retired academic	An avid gardener	A has a moral objection to B	Beach town
2	An auto mechanic	A stay-at-home grandparent	A is B's estranged cousin	State Fair
3	A crime suspect	A part time minister	A and B are both mid-divorce	Fast Food Restaurant
4	A tarot card reader	A financial advisor	Family and friends disapprove of the match between A and B	Opera House
5	A substitute teacher	An unappreciated sculptor	A and B have opposing politics	Apartment complex
6	A lawyer	A meditation guru	A believes B once cheated them of a large sum	Hospital
7	A bored former dentist	A short-order cook	A and B dated in high school	National Park

With these characters in this setting, make your story as outrageous as possible. Write for ten minutes, no stopping, no editing.

Onward to define main characters that flesh out your premise.

CHAPTER 4
CREATE YOUR MAIN CHARACTERS

The **main characters** in a Romance meet in the first act of the story, endure various conflicts and plot twists as their romantic connection develops, and finally overcome their distrust and get together at the happy ending.

The main characters spend most of the story ambivalent about each other. There are things about each that attract the other and things about each that repel the other. Plus each of the main characters has their own internal conflict, often based on their history (backstory), that makes them averse to romance. In the end, of course, love conquers all—but only after a lot of drama.

To build the main characters who will do this dance, you'll need to decide:

- What are each character's attractive qualities?
- What are each character's traits that the other main character finds unappealing, or even repellant?
- What is each character's inner wound or conflict?
- Why do they distrust one another?

Keep those questions in mind as we create each character step by step.

First, let's choose a name for your Character A. Here are some names that were popular in the 1950s, when many of our Well-Seasoned Characters might have been born. For more choices, look at US Census data online for decades that interest you. And with the magic of the Search and Replace function, you can easily change your characters' names later as you edit (just be sure to catch any glitches when you proofread).

CHARACTER NAME: CHOOSE A NAME THAT SUITS YOUR CHARACTER (OR CHOOSE A NAME AT RANDOM)

Example Female Names		Example Male Names	
Diane	Carol	Andy	Rodney
Harriet	Susan	Stanley	Hugo
Ellen	Rose	Larry	Harvey
Suzanne	Sharon	Gregory	Jay
Ginger	Robin	Rudy	Timothy
Lynn	Darlene	Gary	Matteo
Janet	Joan	Henry	Theo
Helen	Frances	Leroy	Louis
April	Joyce	Anthony	Sidney

I focus on female names that end with a consonant and male names that end with a vowel, just to mess with gender expectations. If that's not your jam, or to find more gender-neutral names, baby name lists are your friend. Try searching for common names by decade of birth.

Now that your Character A has a name, we will interview them to learn more about them. Imagine you are chatting in a coffee shop with your newly named Helen or Henry. It is helpful to find a photo that looks like your character and keep that in front of you while you capture the conversation. The photo can be from a magazine or search an online photo site like Pixabay.

WRITING CRAFT: CREATE A CHARACTER BACKSTORY VIA INTERVIEW

Use your memories and imagination to create one of your main characters. Your character can be a composite of several people you've known in your life, with the appearance of one, for example, and the interests of another.

Interview the character to learn as much as you can. Below are questions to consider. Feel free to skip questions that do not appeal to you, and if possible, **answer at least one question from each category**.

> Pro Tip: Type your answers on a computer, so that you can copy and paste excerpts from your backstory into your manuscript later as needed.

Key Questions for a Romance Character

- In what ways is your character satisfied, and dissatisfied, with her life right now?
- What does your character fear? How does she compensate (mask her fear)?
- What does your character most want? This can be a secret, known only to her or to her sidekick, that will be disclosed to the reader at the right moment.

Age and Wisdom

- How old is your character at the time of your story?
- In your character's voice, write about three significant events in her life so far.

- What advice would your character give to her younger self?
- How does your character push back on her internalized biases, including ageism, ableism, and size prejudice?

Desires and Secrets

- What makes your character get out of bed in the morning?
- What does she want that she does not admit to anyone?

Appearance and Physical Body

- What does your character look like? Write about her eyes, hair, body type.
- What is her favorite form of movement? How often does she engage in it?
- What is her favorite food?
- How is her body different now than it was twenty years ago?

Self-Image

- What are your character's four favorite things about herself (including about her body)?
- What embarrasses your character about herself?
- How does she get in her own way?
- What social messages about herself does she accept, or reject?

History

- What was her childhood like?
- What youthful experiences (positive and negative) were key to making her who she is today?

- Where did she grow up and where does she live now? (Geographic location and type of dwelling)
- Has she been married, and is she married at the time of your story?
- What challenge did your character overcome in her youth?
- What was (or is) her career? How does she feel about that career?

Social and Family Life

- How sociable is she? What are her favorite ways to socialize?
- Does she have a partner? Is she dating? Does she want to date?
- Does she have children? Grandchildren? Nieces and nephews?
- What does she admire in her friends?
- What do her friends like about her?

Spiritual Life

- Does she have a spiritual or religious practice? Does she practice it regularly?
- What legacy would she like to leave in the world?
- What kind of humor makes her laugh out loud?

Inner Wounds Become Plot Drivers in a Romance

Now that you know this character better, it's time for deeper questions:

- Which of your character's inner wounds or conflicts make them averse to a committed romance?

- What in your character's history explains her inner wound or conflict?

Here you have an advantage as a writer of Seasoned Romance. Your character has had a lifetime to become disillusioned, lose faith in others, or decide they no longer can find love. Or your character may be driven to accomplish an important goal while there is still time, and romance may seem like a distraction. These challenges are great material for a Well-Seasoned Romance.

EXAMPLE OF CHARACTER HISTORY AS SOURCE OF CONFLICT

In *Vampires of a Certain Age*, FDA inspector Rachel Sutter is committed to find the truth about the blood bank owned by the secretive vampire Marion Chase.

> "This lab is only half the size of the upstairs. What else is down here?" Rachel waited. Marion did not speak. "Well? You have a lot of explaining to do. Now, Dr. Chase, why don't you tell me what is really happening here. To whom are you selling old and contaminated blood?"

But after centuries in hiding, Marion is committed to secrecy.

Meanwhile Rachel's childhood in a religious cult has made her skeptical of anything supernatural—including vampires. Here is Rachel's reaction when Marion finally confides in her:

> Rachel threw up her hands. "You expect me to believe this crazy story? That you're not human, not even alive? You don't understand who you're dealing with. I do not believe in life after death. I do not believe in the Resurrection. Certainly not the resurrection of a blood bank owner in a backwater town."

Yet Marion must believe in her own experience and her own body, no matter that she is a scientist and science as it stands can shed no light on her existence.

> "You want data?" Marion brought the scalpel down straight into the palm of her left hand, then pulled it out again. She held it up for Rachel to see. No blood. And the cut had sealed instantly, leaving no trace.
>
> She handed the scalpel to Rachel. "Your turn."
>
> "No. No, I won't."
>
> "Just do it. Otherwise you won't believe me."
>
> Rachel looked Marion in the eye as she stabbed. She felt the point go into Marion's flesh. Rachel looked down, expecting blood.
>
> Not one drop.
>
> "There you have it," said Marion. "Data."

Below are some of the traits that may interfere with a character engaging in a romance. Which of these hold true for the characters in your imagination?

EXAMPLES OF INNER WOUNDS AND CONFLICTS FOR ROMANCE CHARACTERS

1. Fear of Commitment	10. Anxiety
2. Grudge Holding	11. Self-righteousness
3. Prudery	12. Greed
4. Impetuousness	13. Vanity
5. Bluntness	14. Defensiveness
6. Sense of Entitlement	15. Self-Pity
7. The Need for Control	16. Suppressed Rage
8. Dishonesty	17. Hypocrisy
9. Self-Denial	18. Suspiciousness

What about Your Other Main Character?

You just learned a lot about Character A. But what about Character B? These main characters need to attract each other and yet maintain their ambivalence for most of your story.

Go back and repeat the naming and interview process. Start with choosing a name for Character B. As you consider the history and traits of your other main character, keep in mind how the main characters' interlocking traits will shape your story. For example, Character A may be impetuous while Character B is the slow and steady type. Character A may be inclined to panic while Character B's favorite saying is, "Keep Calm and Carry On." At the same time, your two characters should have traits that are mutually attractive in order to create the approach/avoidance pattern in Act Two of a Romance.

Examples of Traits That Could Be Mutually Attractive

- Both main characters love the same thing: books, science, grandchildren, etc.
- Each character is drawn to different things in the other, e.g., Character A loves Character B's sense of humor; Character B admires Character A's community service.

- Mutual physical attraction may play a role here, but there must be more to explore about their personal traits.

Examples of Interlocking Traits That Could Lead to Ambivalence

Some of the classic interlocking traits work across the age spectrum.

- Character A fears abandonment; Character B fears intimacy.
- Character A is cerebral and disdains action; Character B is active and disdains the intellect.

Here are examples that may resonate especially well for older characters.

- The two characters may have known each other half a century ago in high school or college and may have very different memories of how they parted.
- Internalized ageism and ableism may affect how one or both characters see their own body, leading to shame and reluctance to be intimate.

Counter-Tropes and Your Romance Characters

By centering a Romance on characters after midlife, your writing counters ageism in a fresh and creative way. If you choose, you can do even more by constructing characters using *counter tropes*: themes that fly in the face of stereotypes. Here are some examples to consider:

- What if one of your main characters likes their own appearance after fifty more than when they were younger?
- What if one of your main characters has more success at dating after fifty than ever before?

- What if one of your main characters achieves their biggest career success after age sixty? Consider fields that emphasize appearance, like acting or modeling. Or create a character who goes in a new direction and becomes an entrepreneur in their sixties.
- What if one of your main characters becomes an older influencer on social media?
- What if a female main character who has been straight all her life falls in love with a woman?
- What if a monogamous main character becomes polyamorous after sixty?
- Or on the other hand, what if a main character with multiple lovers falls in love with a confirmed monogamist?

These hypotheticals are based on people I've known. What about the people *you* know? Why not create a myth-busting character for your novel?

By now you have a premise for your novel, and you have created two main characters. Think about your story from each main character's viewpoint: What will the story look like to each of them? How will their goals be achieved?

WRITING CRAFT: CHARACTER ARCS IN THE ROMANCE GENRE

A key tool to understanding characters is to build each character's *story arc*. While there is one overarching plot in any story, each character also has their own story within the larger story. This is the story as if told from that character's viewpoint. What does each character want, and do they get it? What stumbling blocks do they overcome along the way?

The *arc* is the character's own personal plot in the story. For the main characters in a Romance, the arc is the result of:

- The nature of the character (as discovered through writing the character backstory) — including their inner wound or conflict.
- The interactions of the character with the other main character (and that character's flaws). These interactions generate the Romance plot.
- How the character grows and changes during the story.
- The external circumstances and how they affect the character (more about that in the External Plot chapter).

While you may tell the story mostly from the point of view of one character, every character in a story has their own viewpoint. The sidekicks and the characters driving the external plot have their own arcs and backstories. But let's begin with the main characters A and B.

- In a Romance, the main characters will have a positive growth arc, meaning they end up happier than they were at the beginning of the story.

You have already outlined the starting point for each character:

- The character has several strong points.
- The character has an inner wound or conflict.

The character arc will progress in the middle of the story:

- The character alternately takes risks and retreats.

And, finally, the character arc will resolve:

- The character overcomes their inner wounds or flaws and takes a chance on love.

A diagram of that process looks like this:

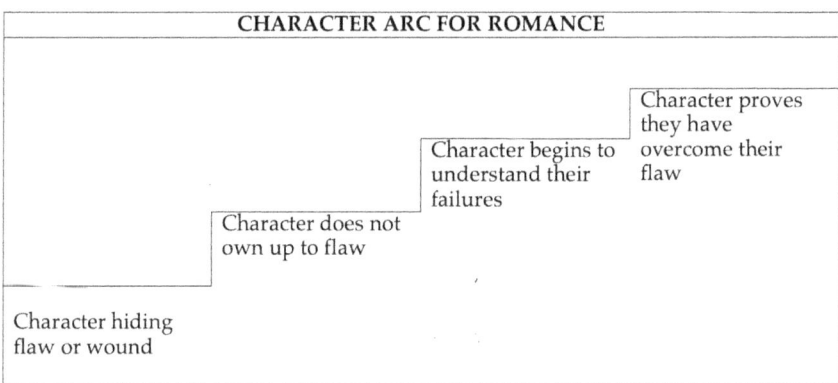

What that arc looks like for each character determines what the overall plot will look like. Here is an example: the character arc for Marion Chase, Character A in *Vampires of a Certain Age*.

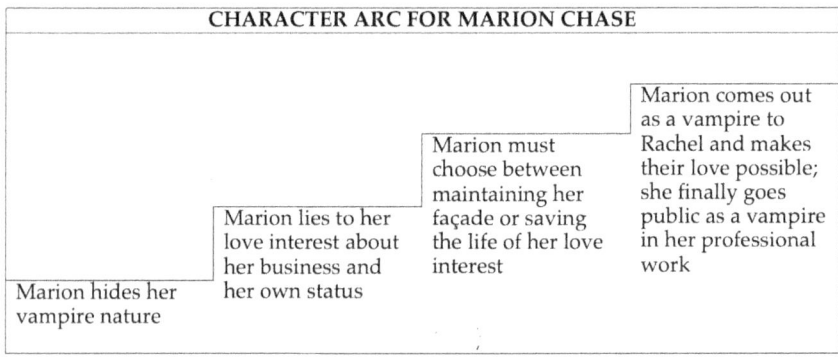

Try building an arc for one of your main characters. But first, try the two Quick Write Exercises below.

QUICK WRITING EXERCISE #1: SHOW VERSUS TELL IN CHARACTER DEVELOPMENT

Actions speak louder than words in fiction as in life. If Character A is anxious, having them check the stove twice or even three times when they leave the house shows the reader that trait more convincingly than announcing it in narrative.

Choose a trait you discovered when you interviewed a main character. Write down three ways you might *show* that trait to the reader instead of *telling* them.

QUICK WRITING EXERCISE #2: GENERATE CONFLICT

By now you have a good idea of your story premise and who your main characters are. And we've talked about the ambiguity, the back-and-forth, between the main characters as they alternately approach and run away from their loving relationship. Now take five minutes to brainstorm a list of possible conflicts (big and small) that could be short-term barriers to love in your story. You'll need both big and little reasons for your characters to run away from each other when it's time to develop your plot. Be sure to save your list. No idea is too silly. Ready, set, write!

In the next chapter we will explore how to create a sidekick character for each of the main characters that will add depth to your story.

CHAPTER 5
CREATE SIDEKICK CHARACTERS

In a Romance, where the story revolves around the relationship between the main characters, it is useful to the writer for each of the two main characters to have a **sidekick**—a confidant to commiserate with about the ups and downs of the romance. The sidekick might be a sibling, an old friend, or a protégé. In this chapter we will explore the ways you can employ these sidekick characters to achieve your story goals.

The sidekick is also the keeper of the main character's history including their romantic motivations and fears. For example:

- A sidekick could worry that his younger brother will never again find love—because his brother *believes* he was betrayed by the love of his life years earlier.
- The sidekick could be a longtime colleague who knows her friend is afraid she will lose her professional edge if she gets involved—because that happened to her years before.
- The sidekick could be the keeper of an important family secret that they only reveal to the main character in the midst of the novel.

The sidekick should have a stake in the outcome of the story: an *opinion* about the main character's relationship and a *role* in making it happen (or trying to stop it). The sidekick can provide:

- comic relief when the main character takes it all too seriously.
- a shoulder to cry on when there's a crisis.
- a call for improvement when the main character can't see their own flaws, and, importantly,
- revelation of key backstory that the reader needs to know.

The sidekick should be distinct enough from the main character to give a different perspective. He or she may see their shared history differently and may be more optimistic (or more pessimistic) about the romance developing between the main characters. You may wish to interview your sidekick characters, as you did for your main characters in Chapter Four. These interviews can be less in-depth than the ones you conducted for your main characters but can still provide insights into their motivations and how they will contribute to the plot.

In my novel, *Vampires of a Certain Age*, Marion Chase is a 500-year-old vampire who runs a blood bank with a side business of supplying ethically sourced blood to vampires. Marion's sidekick, Amber Pettis, is a young mortal who is Marion's righthand woman. At first, Amber knows nothing of the secret mission of the blood bank. As Marion gradually introduces Amber to the role of the night shift, the reader learns more about Marion's true nature. The scene below sets up Marion's character to reveal part of her backstory to her second-in-command.

SIDEKICK / MAIN CHARACTER INTERACTION FROM *VAMPIRES OF A CERTAIN AGE*

AMBER (A SIDEKICK CHARACTER) PRODS MARION (A MAIN CHARACTER) TO REVEAL HER BACKSTORY.

Amber perched on one arm of the couch, a glass of ruby red wine in her hand, and gestured to Marion. "Sit. Have a glass of—no, you won't have wine, will you?"

"No thanks," said Marion.

"So. Why don't you eat? Or drink?"

"You won't let this go, will you?"

"Nope."

Marion sighed. "Oh, alright. I drink blood."

Amber stared at her for a second and then burst out laughing. "Sure, you do."

Marion didn't laugh. "I can't believe I said that."

"Because it's baloney."

"No; it's true. But I know better than to say it."

Amber stopped laughing. "So when you told me you'd been on a diet for five hundred years—"

"I wasn't exaggerating."

"Are you telling me you're a—"

"Vampire. The word you want is vampire."

"Oh, come on. You're yanking my chain."

"No. I'm not."

"Alright. Tell me—"

"How I came to be one?"

"No. How your immune system works. As a dead person."

Marion laughed. "That's a new one."

"I'm serious. If you're 'undead,' or whatever you call it, how do you fight off disease?" Amber sipped her wine. "Inquiring minds want to know."

"I have no idea. I've had other fish to fry this last half millennium."

"Like what?"

"*Like surviving. And helping others of my kind survive.*"
"*Surviving. As a vampire.*"
"*Yes.*"
"*Alright, I'll bite.*" Amber laughed at her own accidental joke. "*How, exactly, did you become a vampire?*"

Marion stared at nothing. "*It's hard to remember that far back. But I know that my house was on fire.*"

QUICK WRITING EXERCISE: A HELPFUL SIDEKICK

Reflect on someone in your life who picked you up when you were down. That person is a potential model for one of your sidekick characters. Write about them for twenty minutes, no stopping or editing.

Sidekicks Can Add Depth and Conflict

The sidekick offers plenty of opportunity to introduce conflict to the story. This is especially true in a Well-Seasoned Romance where a main character and sidekick may have history that stretches back for decades. Consider a few of the possibilities:

- What if the sidekick is secretly in love with the main character and has an ulterior motive for trashing the potential new love?
- What if the sidekick is harboring a grudge from something that happened decades ago, and sabotaging the main character's romance is a chance for revenge?
- What if the sidekick is in love with the other sidekick?
- What if the sidekick is in love with the other main character?
- What if the sidekick knows a secret about the main character and threatens to reveal it to the love interest?

In *Vampires of a Certain Age*, Marion Chase's sidekick, Amber Pettis, pretends to be attracted to the other main character's sidekick (a junior FDA inspector) to distract him from discovering that the blood bank provides rejected blood to Midwestern vampires. Over time, Amber develops authentic feelings for Luke, who is attracted to her but skeptical about her feelings. The push-pull between the sidekick characters develops into a secondary Enemies-to-Lovers Romance plot, complete with betrayal. In this scene, Luke is having dinner with his boss, Rachel, when he becomes convinced that Amber is lying to him.

A Sidekick Betrayal in *Vampires of a Certain Age*

Luke looked out the window at the scene in the well-lit parking lot and the blood drained from his face.
"What's wrong?"
"Oh. Nothing. It's just Amber, kissing some long-haired guy."
Rachel glanced out the window. Amber was clearly having a good time. "I'm sorry, Luke. But this proves that she's been leading you on—in the same way that Marion is leading me on. It could be a deliberate distraction. A strategy. A way to take our attention away from the fact that they are hiding something."
Luke was still staring at Amber. "Yes. I didn't want to believe it. I thought she liked me. But there it is."

Lots of plot-enriching mischief can be had with these supporting characters. In *Vampires of a Certain Age*, Dr. Marion Chase's sidekick, Amber, helps her boss keep the secret of where the night staff prepares rejected blood for vampires. Then, just as the reader thinks that Luke and Amber might get together, Amber accidentally reveals the underground location to Luke.

A Sidekick Almost-Love Scene from V*ampires of a Certain Age*

On a whim, he opened the door of the supply closet and beckoned her inside. She hesitated just for a moment, then came in and closed the door. Her scent was all around him, his arms were all around her. Her hair under his hands was smooth as cornsilk and as he embraced her she felt to him like the most perfect being who ever was. His lips found hers, and hers were soft, giving, and he pulled her close, his eyes closed, his body curved slightly to accommodate her shorter stature. His hands slipped under the back of her blouse and now he felt the skin of her back, just as smooth. He could barely believe that he got to hold her, and kiss her, and—just then he opened his eyes for a moment, and with his eyes now adjusted to the darkness he saw a line of light underneath the top shelf of the supply cabinet.

He stopped kissing her. "What is that?" He let go of her.

"What is what?"

"That light. Very dim, just there. That line of light, across the bottom of this shelf."

"I don't see a light."

"No, you wouldn't. It's above that shelf that's over your head. I think there's a door here."

"Oh! No, there can't be. You've seen the floorplans."

"Yes, of course." The floorplans. The ones that failed to show the extra air vents. The air vents that could serve an undisclosed basement. "You are so lovely," he said, resuming his caresses.

"Thank you," she said. "You're not bad yourself."

"We should probably go, though, before things get out of hand."

"Aren't they already?"

He chuckled. "Not as much as they could be. Come, let me walk you to your car."

They walked to the front door, closer than two people should be who were only acquaintances, but not arm in arm, just in case they met someone. He held the front door open for her. "Where are you parked?"

"Right here."

"I'll say goodnight, then." He kissed her, still holding the door open. "Mind if I go back in? Just need to visit the men's room for a second."

She hesitated. She could hardly demand to accompany him into the men's room, and how odd it would be to insist on protocol when they had just kissed.

"I'll come right back out, I promise," he said. "No bodyguard needed."

She laughed. "See you tomorrow."

"See you then." *He waved as she drove away, then turned and headed back to the closet.*

There had to be a latch somewhere. And there was.

In Chapter Two, "Creating Main Characters" you developed a full history, or **backstory**, for each of your main characters. Creating backstories gives your characters depth on the page. Even if you don't ultimately use every detail in the story, the presence of that history gives you the freedom to explore many options in your writing.

WRITING CRAFT: HOW TO USE BACKSTORY

The interplay between each main character and their sidekick is a great way to introduce character history. A conversation with a sidekick about what's happening in the story can be a natural place for a piece of backstory if the sidekick believes the main character's concerns or actions are based on their history. That history can illustrate how the main character developed their traits, including their hesitation to commit to a relationship.

We've all read fiction that inserts too much backstory in dialogue —when one character tells another things they would already know. Don't worry about this in your first draft; for now, it's fine to "dump" backstory. You will have plenty of time to edit later. When you come back to edit, you can "drip" various parts of your characters' backstories with care, when it's a natural part of the story—much as a person in real life might confide a piece of their history when it's relevant. As you write your first draft, do try hinting around about something in a character's past (foreshadowing), and leave the reader wondering for a while.

You can also include a flashback scene to share part of the backstory. A main character can reflect internally on a key memory, prompted by a comment from their sidekick or by another trigger in the story.

WRITING EXERCISE: SIDEKICKS AND BACKSTORIES

Revisit the previous chapter on "Creating Main Characters" and choose names for your sidekick characters. Then use prompts from the Interview exercise in that chapter to develop each of your sidekick characters. Create backstories for your sidekick characters. These may be less detailed than for your mains but should include how they met their respective main characters.

With these understandings of premise, character and setting, let's construct your compelling Romance plot.

CHAPTER 6
BUILD THE ROMANCE PLOT

The **plot** is the series of actions in a story. Plot is driven by conflicts within and between characters, and by external events. Often described as an arc, plot rises to a peak or climax, and then resolves at the end of the story. *In a Romance novel, the primary driver of the plot is conflict about the romantic relationship.*

The plot starts with the **setup** of the story (Act One), which begins by showing the reader the life each main character is living before the two meet. After the main characters are introduced individually to the reader, they are introduced to each other. In Romance, the setup focuses on the "meet cute," which is the first encounter of the main characters, often a humorous or awkward encounter. The Romance setup also hints at the inner conflicts of the main characters as a preview to the interpersonal conflicts ahead. Those inner conflicts will make it difficult for the characters to commit to a relationship later in the story. We will explore this opening part of the novel in greater depth in Chapter Eight.

In the **central section** (Act Two) of a novel, the action is driven by conflicts that arise between the characters and from external events. In Romance, the primary conflicts relate to the romantic relationship between the main characters. The conflicts based on external events are the primary drivers of most fiction but are secondary drivers of a Romance plot. The action in Act Two rises until the crisis, when the characters seek to resolve the main conflict. In the Romance genre, the crisis of the story involves the breakdown of the main characters' romance. More on this in Chapters Nine and Ten.

The **resolution** of the story occurs in Act Three. While many types of resolution can occur in novels, a defining trait of the Romance genre is the happy ending, when characters resolve their differences and commit to their relationship. To reach that end, the characters must own and resolve their internal conflicts, often with assistance from their respective sidekick characters. This healing of inner wounds enables the main characters to trust each other and become effective romantic partners. External conflicts, while also resolved, are less important in a Romance novel. Explore this Romance resolution in Chapter Eleven.

This basic storyline is repeated over and over in this perennially popular genre. The Romance plot has to be one of the most satisfying storylines the human psyche ever invented, because humans have an insatiable appetite for stories that fit this pattern.

QUICK WRITING EXERCISE: STORY OVERVIEW

It's useful to look at other writers' work for perspective on story elements. In this exercise, choose one of your favorite Seasoned Romance stories. It could be a novel or a movie (Examples of Well-Seasoned Romance books and movies are listed in the Resources at the end of Part One). Please write down:

- The premise.
- The inner conflicts of the two main characters.
- The external conflict.
- The basis for the attraction between the two main characters.

- A quick summary of the beginning, the middle and the end of the story.

In coming chapters we will explore in detail each of the three Acts within a Romance, and you will be offered writing exercises to assist in building your three act structure. In the remainder of this chapter, we will look at types of conflict and at the overall plot structure.

INTERNAL AND EXTERNAL CONFLICT

Without conflict there is no story. If two people meet in high school, fall in love, and live together in harmony for the rest of their lives, that is great for them but it's not the basis for a gripping story.

There are two main forms of conflict: Internal and external. In most fiction the *external conflict* drives the story. Romance, if there is one, is secondary. In the Romance genre, *internal conflict* and its resolution drive the story because the romance plot is the main plot. However, the external plot can be a catalyst for the romance plot (as in stories such as *Romeo and Juliet* where two people from opposing groups fall in love). The chart below shows the differences between internal and external conflict.

COMPARISON OF INTERNAL AND EXTERNAL CONFLICTS

Internal Conflict:	External Conflict:
<ul><li>Conflict is centered within a main character's mind</li><li>May be based on events in the character's past that create a hidden wound or character flaw</li><li>Internal conflict influences the character's response to the possibility of a relationship</li><li>In the Romance genre, this internal conflict must be resolved for the relationship to succeed</li><li>A supporting character (sidekick) may help the main character come to grips with the inner conflict</li><li>The internal conflict must be resolved before the happy ending</li></ul>	<ul><li>Conflict is between main character(s) and an outside force (for example, a space alien, a fire, an epidemic)</li><li>Outside force may be an event, another character, or both</li><li>The outside force may reveal the true nature(s) of the main character(s)</li><li>In Romance, the conflict with an outside force may catalyze a relationship (e.g., two single people in a pandemic lock down together for companionship)</li><li>The external conflict is likely resolved around the same time in the story as the internal conflicts of the main characters</li></ul>

QUICK WRITING EXERCISE:

- Review the *inner conflict* of a character you interviewed. Write down possible ways to resolve that inner conflict. Write for ten minutes, no stopping, no editing.
- Write about the inner conflict of your other main character.
- List alternative plot developments that could resolve that inner conflict.

Three Act Structure for Your Romance

As described above, the Romance novel typically follows the classic three act structure, with a beginning, a middle and an end. Setting up that structure before you begin writing will help you write material that moves your story in the direction it needs to go.

In the template below, the middle of the story (which is typically the longest part) is further divided into Act Two Part One and Act Two Part Two. As an example, the plot outline for *Vampires of a Certain Age* is filled in.

PLOT OUTLINE FOR *VAMPIRES OF A CERTAIN AGE*

Act One	1. **Introduce A and B separately (before they meet)** *Introduces Marion as an herbal healer in medieval England and then as a modern blood bank executive. Introduces Rachel as a successful senior FDA inspector.*	2. **The "Meet Cute"** *Marion sees Rachel and is instantly reminded of her first love centuries ago. Rachel meets Marion and knows she has met her match in this adversary — and wonders at Marion's resemblance to a photo of a long-dead scientist.*	3. **A and B thrown together by circumstance** *The two main characters must interact as polite adversaries throughout the blood bank inspection.*
Act Two Part One	4. **Challenge from External Plot** *The inspection reveals clues about the hidden second business at the blood bank — clues that Rachel cannot quite make sense of.*	5. **A and B glimpse each other's inner qualities** *Rachel and Marion are drawn to each other by their savvy and their assertiveness.*	6. **False High (or False Low)** *Rachel becomes convinced that Marion is flirting with her to distract Rachel from Marion's wrongdoing at the blood bank. This repels Rachel.*
Act Two Part Two	7. **Inner Conflicts Lead to Rising Fear** *Marion's need to protect her service to other vampires is in conflict with her deep attraction to Rachel; Rachel's deep distrust of everything but data leads her to distrust her own feelings (and Marion).*	8. **Worst Fears Realized / Betrayal** *Rachel discovers the hidden basement and concludes Marion is selling contaminated blood, endangering the public.*	9. **Breakup** *Rachel tries to call in law enforcement to arrest Marion, but is overcome by her own serious illness.*
Act Three	10. **Decision to Resolve Inner Conflicts** *Marion sacrifices the secrecy about her mission to save Rachel; Rachel becomes a vampire and learns the real reason for Marion's secrecy.*	11. **Climax / Happy Ending** *With both main characters now immortal, and now that Rachel understands the reason for Marion's hidden business, the two become lovers.*	12. **(Optional) Epilogue** *Rachel reunites with her children in England; both main characters visit Marion's 16th century cottage. They make plans to found a new institute to study vampire biology.*

Practice filling in a chart with an outline of a favorite Seasoned Romance novel or movie. Then begin to develop the plot for your Well-Seasoned Romance by completing the second chart in this writing exercise.

STELLA FOSSE

WRITING EXERCISE: PLOT OVERVIEW FOR A WELL-SEASONED ROMANCE

Please fill in this template with an outline for a Romance novel or movie you have enjoyed. For a downloadable copy you can fill in on your computer, please go to https://stellafosse.com/wsrdownload.

Act One	1. Introduce A and B separately (before they meet)	2. The "Meet Cute"	3. A and B thrown together by circumstance
Act Two Part One	4. Challenge from External Plot	5. A and B glimpse each other's inner qualities	6. False High (or False Low)
Act Two Part Two	7. Inner Conflicts Lead to Rising Fear	8. Worst Fears Realized / Betrayal	9. Breakup
Act Three	10. Decision to Resolve Inner Conflicts	11. Climax / Happy Ending	12. (Optional) Epilogue

WRITING EXERCISE: PLOT OVERVIEW FOR YOUR WELL-SEASONED ROMANCE

Act One	1. Introduce A and B separately (before they meet)	2. The "Meet Cute"	3. A and B thrown together by circumstance
Act Two Part One	4. Challenge from External Plot	5. A and B glimpse each other's inner qualities	6. False High (or False Low)
Act Two Part Two	7. Inner Conflicts Lead to Rising Fear	8. Worst Fears Realized / Betrayal	9. Breakup
Act Three	10. Decision to Resolve Inner Conflicts	11. Climax / Happy Ending	12. (Optional) Epilogue

Now brainstorm several possible plots with the template above and pick your favorite. If you choose to write your novel about one of these story ideas, modify as you wish while writing your story—this exercise is a jumping off place for your writing and can change as you go, as long as your story adheres to the Romance structure. For a downloadable copy you can fill in on your computer, please go to https://stellafosse.com/wsrdownload.

In addition to a well structured Romance plot, building romantic tension throughout your story will be key to the success of your novel. In the craft section below, consider how that tension will begin and then continue to grow throughout your story.

WRITING CRAFT: BUILDING ROMANTIC TENSION

A Romance novel is a lengthy seduction. It is sensual by nature. Long before an intimate love scene, you can convey the sensuality of the story by evoking the senses. What do your characters smell, hear, see, touch and taste when they are together? Do they share delicious food? Walk in an aromatic garden? The setting of your story is deeply connected with the senses.

To support a powerful resolution in Act Three, the romantic tension between the main characters must start early and keep building throughout Act Two. The alternation of attraction and conflict also generates romantic tension. When one character is busy running away, the other is free to feel their attraction more fully.

As you flesh out your characters and your plot overview, consider how your characters' emotional and physical connection will progress over time, beginning with initial awareness and leading to a love scene or scenes later in the story. Here is one scenario for the stages of mutual seduction:

- Awareness of physical nearness.
- Eye contact.
- Verbal contact.
- Hand to hand contact.
- Arm to arm, as when sitting closely.
- Light kiss.
- Touching hair.
- Touching the body.

Plan how you will build that tension for your characters. Look back at the Three Act Structure you just created and write down roughly where the various stages of heightening physical contact might occur.

None of this stops your seasoned characters from falling into bed before they fall in love. People over sixty have one-night stands too, and sometimes a one-night stand blossoms into a love affair (after many twists and turns, of course). But if your characters enjoy an initial encounter, that rendezvous should include not just lust, but also an emotional component and a hint of more to come.

AUTOFICTION QUICK WRITE:

Think about a time when you had a big crush on someone. Remember that experience in a detailed, sensory way. Write for ten minutes, no stopping, no editing.

Build that intensity into one of your main characters.

In this chapter we have focused primarily on the internal plot, the main engine of any genre Romance. In the next chapter we will step back and look at the drivers of the external plot.

CHAPTER 7
BUILD THE EXTERNAL PLOT FOR YOUR ROMANCE NOVEL

In a Romance novel, the key plot is internal: the vagaries of the romance between the two main characters. But while it is secondary to that internal plot, the **external plot** adds richness and complexity to your Romance novel. It is also a place where your life experience can shine.

What is an External Plot?

The external plot is just what it sounds like: a series of events outside the characters' direct control, in the physical environment of the story. The external plot can make it harder for the main characters to develop their romantic attachment, for reasons beyond their emotional issues. These reasons could include conflicts with other characters (such as meddlesome adult children) and challenges with outside institutions (such as an employer or volunteer organization).

While an external plot can add to the depth of your story, make sure it aligns with the internal plot. For example, if the external plot physically separates your characters permanently from one another, you story will be derailed—unless a plot twist brings them back together after they have time to realize how much they miss one another.

Let's look at potential source material for the external plot of your novel.

WRITING EXERCISE: EXTERNAL CONFLICT

Make a list of possible conflicts based on the ideas below.

Look back on your career and consider real or plausible conflict situations that could give rise to a plot.

- Were you (or are you) in corporate life? Consider rivalries, interpersonal drama, bonding about wretched bosses.
- Have you been involved in a layoff? How did people react —both those who left and those who stayed?
- What else stands out about your work experience? (For example, I will always remember when a colleague was arrested for putting out a contract on his wife.)

What hobbies or interests have you developed that can generate storylines?

- Are you a theater buff? Lots of drama in that arena.
- Do you collect rocks? What about competition for samples, and surprising discoveries in the field?
- What really stands out about your hobbies or interests over the years?

What notable events in your community have occurred during your lifetime?

- Is there an event or series of events that could become an external plot?

- This could include the effects of a natural disaster.

From your list, choose a few of these conflicts that sound most intriguing. Then use these techniques to develop your ideas further:

- Consider how to *raise the stakes*: Think of three ways to make the conflict more significant.
- How would this external conflict bring the main characters together? Push them apart?
- What is forbidden? How would this external conflict get in the way of the romance?

From the options you're considering, choose the external conflict that:

- Fits your characters best, and
- Has the most potential to add intrigue and excitement to your story.

The next step is to take a promising *external conflict* and develop it into the outline of an *external plot,* as in the exercise below.

WRITING EXERCISE: OUTLINE A FULL EXTERNAL PLOT

Although everything is subject to change while you write, it is helpful to set off on your writing adventure with a clear idea of where you are going. This is especially true in a structured genre such as Romance. That means creating a three act outline for your external plot before you write, beginning with an inciting incident, continuing through the conflicts of Act Two, and ending with a resolution for your external plot that supports the happy ending. Here is an example External Plot outline from my novel, *Vampires of a Certain Age:*

EXTERNAL PLOT OUTLINE FOR *VAMPIRES OF A CERTAIN AGE*

The external plot involves the sequence of an FDA inspection.

Act One	Act Two Part One	Act Two Part Two	Act Three
External Plot Event Brings Characters A and B Together	External Plot Events Generate Conflict	External Plot Events Contribute to Breakup	External Plot is Resolved in a Way that Supports Happy Ending
FDA inspectors arrive at a blood bank that is surreptitiously feeding Midwestern vampires.	Inspection raises questions: Some blood bank activities seem to make no sense or are against regulations.	Inspectors discover the hidden basement and a supply of expired and rejected blood.	With the senior inspector, Rachel, now officially dead, the junior inspector (Luke) files an inspection report with only minor infractions. He goes on to inspect and excuse other blood banks that service vampires.

Next, outline the external plot of a favorite Romance novel or film (see the list at the end of Part One for suggestions). For a downloadable copy of this chart that you can fill in on your computer, please go to https://stellafosse.com/wsrdownload.

EXTERNAL PLOT OUTLINE FOR A FAVORITE SEASONED ROMANCE

Act One	Act Two Part One	Act Two Part Two	Act Three
External Plot Event Brings Characters A and B Together	External Plot Events Generate Conflict	External Plot Events Contribute to Breakup	External Plot is Resolved in a Way that Supports Happy Ending

And now try outlining an external plot for your own story.

EXTERNAL PLOT OUTLINE FOR YOUR OWN SEASONED ROMANCE

Act One	Act Two Part One	Act Two Part Two	Act Three
External Plot Event Brings Characters A and B Together	External Plot Events Generate Conflict	External Plot Events Contribute to Breakup	External Plot is Resolved in a Way that Supports Happy Ending

To enrich the development of your external plot, let's take another look at Autofiction, which is the blending of our lived experience with our imagination. You can put this technique to great effect.

We always write what we know, and it is typical for a writer's first novel to contain more memory and less imagination than her later books. So why not embrace that evolution by mixing and matching from your own unique experience? A favorite setting from one decade of your life can host a character based on a compelling figure in your memory from a different decade. Choose a conflict that consumed you in yet another part of your life, and make it bigger. Voila! The alchemy of autofiction.

WRITING EXERCISE IN AUTOFICTION:

Imagine someone you know now in an external conflict you faced in your forties and a place where you lived in your twenties, whose love interest is an attractive person you met in your fifties. Now write for twenty minutes, no stopping, no editing.

Now that you have an overview of both your internal and external plot, let's begin a detailed look at constructing each Act in your new Romance novel, beginning at the start of your story.

CHAPTER 8
ACT ONE — WHEN WORLDS COLLIDE

Act One in a Romance novel has two functions: First, show each character immersed in the lives they lead before they meet each other. And second, show the intersection of these two lives.

In a Romance novel, introducing your characters to each other in a memorable way can raise your reader's curiosity and keep them reading. The **meet cute** is their first meeting in a humorous or awkward situation that eventually leads to romance. The meet cute is a staple of romantic comedies in films, where visual elements are key. Two characters meet while buying pajamas and end up with each other's garments. Two characters chase all over Paris and finally meet right in front of the Eiffel Tower. Two characters share a cab from JFK to Manhattan and discover they thoroughly dislike each other. You get the idea. Of course, in a Well-Seasoned Romance, your main characters bring together decades of life experience. It's not so much "Meet Cute" as "When Worlds Collide."

By the end of Act One, both the basis for mutual attraction and the barriers to the relationship (inner and external conflicts, and the resulting lack of trust) should be clear to the reader. Below is an example of a first meeting from *Vampires of a Certain Age*.

STELLA FOSSE

THE MAIN CHARACTERS MEET IN *VAMPIRES OF A CERTAIN AGE*

MARION CHASE AND RACHEL SUTTER BEGIN AS ADVERSARIES.

Dr. Sutter presented the requisite papers, like the ones Marion had seen many times before, and gave the standard spiel. The blood bank was required by law to show all documents on request. Records of acquisition, testing, and disposition of failed or expired blood were all in scope, along with the backgrounds and qualifications of everyone on staff.

"And so," said Rachel, "Let's begin with you, Dr. Chase. Tell us how you came to be head of this blood bank."

Marion was ready with the well-rehearsed pablum of a sanitized life. Just once she longed to tell the whole tale. Especially to this one, who called herself Rachel Sutter; this woman who evoked someone from her past whom Marion did not want to remember.

Marion was accustomed to the stream of faces, variations on a theme from one generation to the next. She could remain in the day, fixed on the task and the people at hand; beyond that, all humans blurred together. The mind can barely contain the memories of one lifetime, much less centuries.

At times a resemblance struck her. A face she passed on the street might conjure a medieval publican, long gone from the citadel at York. Or a store clerk's expression might bring to mind a soldier she nursed in the trenches of France in 1918. But the face of the senior inspector was more than an echo of another life. This was the true likeness of Cecily, the woman she adored in the village of Whixton, centuries ago; the lover Marion wished she could have saved.

In dreams Marion allowed herself to remember Cecily's face. In her waking hours, in her professional life, she would never acknowledge the shock she felt when Rachel Sutter shook her hand.

Breakdown of Act One in a Romance Novel

Act One will take up about a quarter of your novel. In a Romance, Act One has a defined structure.

- First, introduce each of your main characters to the reader before they meet each other. Establish each of them as an independent person with their own goals—AND their own flaws.
- Next, the "meet cute," a memorable first meeting "when worlds collide." For example, one character gets her foot stuck in a train track; the other frees her. Or, one character rear ends the other at a stoplight.

Give your Character A reasons to keep thinking of Character B, and vice versa. Something about them attracts. Introduce a problem right away: opposing views, habits, agendas, or life goals. Hence the push-pull of ambivalence that will keep dramatic tension (and romantic tension) building throughout your novel.

In addition, in Act One you will create an external circumstance that keeps your characters in contact with each other—even when they don't want to be. For example: They are assigned to a project together and cannot avoid each other. Or, for a reason you define, they pretend to be in a relationship. Or their children are exes and so the main characters have the same grandchildren.

After agonizing, one character may take the next step and reach out to the other. In any case, external circumstances require that they are bound together for the length of the story.

As an illustration, here is a summary of Act One for *Vampires of a Certain Age*.

SUMMARY OF ACT ONE FOR *VAMPIRES OF A CERTAIN AGE*

Step Within Act One	Content Suggestions	Steps from Act One of *Vampires of a Certain Age*
1. Introduce Character A	What are his/her goals, life circumstances? Attitudes toward romance? Inner wound/flaw? How to show not tell (through actions, dialogue)?	In 1540, the vampire Vivienne saves herbal healer Marion from a mob; in the process, Marion becomes a vampire. Marion had already lost her first love, Cecily, and channels her loving feelings into rescuing other women—and later, into helping her kind through her blood bank.
2. Introduce Character B	What are his/her goals, life circumstances? Attitudes toward romance? Inner wound/flaw? How to show not tell (through actions, dialogue)?	Rachel is a successful senior FDA inspector. Raised in a Christian fundamentalist cult, she is skeptical of anything she cannot see or measure. After the death of her partner she became even more career focused. And in the absence of her grown children (who live in England), Rachel treats her junior inspector, Luke, like a son.
3. The "Meet Cute"	First meeting. We already know why they will be in conflict, and what will attract them.	Rachel arrives to inspect Marion's Chicago blood bank. The two natural adversaries are savvy, incisive women who are inconveniently attracted to one another. They are impressed with each other and wary of one another.
4. Turning Point	They are thrown together for the duration of the story. One character decides to reach out and starts the push and pull dynamic of the story.	Marion flirts with Rachel, convincing herself that it's only to distract Rachel from the inspection, when really Marion and Rachel are mutually attracted. Rachel distances herself, certain that Marion's flirting is a ruse.

WRITING EXERCISE FOR ACT ONE STRUCTURE:

Fill in the Act One breakdown below for a favorite Romance story. For a downloadable copy of this chart that you can fill in on your computer, please go to https://stellafosse.com/wsrdownload.

Step Within Act One	Content Suggestions	Steps for a Favorite Romance
1. Introduce Character A	What are his/her goals, life circumstances? Attitudes toward romance? Inner wound/flaw? How to show not tell (through actions, dialogue)?	
2. Introduce Character B	What are his/her goals, life circumstances? Attitudes toward romance? Inner wound/flaw? How to show not tell (through actions, dialogue)?	
3. The "Meet Cute"	First meeting. We already know why they will be in conflict, and what will attract them.	
4. Turning Point	They are thrown together for the duration of the story. One character decides to reach out (or not) and starts the push and pull dynamic of the story.	

Then brainstorm several versions of your own Act One, based on the characters you have developed. Now create an Act One structure for your own Romance.

Step Within Act One	Content Suggestions	Steps for Your Well-Seasoned Romance
1. Introduce Character A	What are his/her goals, life circumstances? Attitudes toward romance? Inner wound/flaw? How to show not tell (through actions, dialogue)?	
2. Introduce Character B	What are his/her goals, life circumstances? Attitudes toward romance? Inner wound/flaw? How to show not tell (through actions, dialogue)?	
3. The "Meet Cute"	First meeting. We already know why they will be in conflict, and what will attract them.	
4. Turning Point	They are thrown together for the duration of the story. One character decides to reach out (or not) and starts the push and pull dynamic of the story.	

Now that you have constructed your characters and created the structure for the first act of your novel, this is an excellent moment to learn more about writing a scene.

A *scene* is the basic unit of a novel where characters engage in action or dialogue. A chapter usually contains several scenes, each of which has its own beginning, middle and end. In the exercise below, you will write a scene for your Well-Seasoned Romance.

WRITING CRAFT: BUILDING A SCENE

A *scene* is an incident in a larger story. And each finished scene, just like the novel itself, should have:

- A Beginning (setup; can include setting, narrative).
- A Middle (action, conflict, growth, moves story forward).
- An End (which in the case of a scene can be resolution—or a cliffhanger).

As you write and later as you edit, you will construct the story elements for each scene, such as dialogue and setting. Your first draft likely won't address all these elements in each scene. When it's time to edit, you will come back and decide how to fulfill the potential of each scene.

Below are some strategies for scene building.

- Read scenes from Well-Seasoned Romance novels (see Part One Resources), and study how the writer put them together. You can also analyze scenes in Well-Seasoned Romance movies.
- Consider how your characters' motivations lead to decisions in a given chapter. What does the chain of events look like? Then break that chain down into scenes.
- In a given scene, what is each character's goal? How do the characters' goals conflict?
- Think about how you want each scene to begin and end. Some scenes may end with a hook that pulls the reader into the next scene, while others end with a resolution.

> Pro Tip: Ending the last scene in a chapter with a hook (or "cliff-hanger") will keep your readers going from chapter to chapter.

NOTE ABOUT SCENES VERSUS CHAPTERS:

Each chapter in a novel is composed of several scenes. The reader is likely to be more aware of chapters than scenes, but scenes are the most important building blocks of your novel. Though your reader may not consciously notice, your story may be easier to read if your chapters each have roughly the same number of scenes.

In the example scene below, Rachel confirms her suspicions that more is going on than meets the eye at Marion's blood bank. These discoveries continue to build in the remainder of the chapter.

EXAMPLE SCENE FROM *VAMPIRES OF A CERTAIN AGE*

Rachel rounded a corner in the blood bank hallway and saw a lab tech in a white coat walk into the supply closet. She realized that Marion, next to her, was walking just a bit more quickly than usual, speaking more rapidly than usual, as if to distract her. But from what?

"We are looking at a pathogen inactivation process for blood as an additional safeguard, on top of standard testing for infectious diseases. What are your thoughts about those methods?"

Rachel nodded as if listening closely. As they approached the door of the closet, Marion's gestures became broader, as if to draw Rachel's attention. Marion was to her right and the closet door to her left. Without a word, Rachel opened the door of the closet and turned on the light.

"Ah! You can see how we organize our supplies, with those purchased first at the front of each shelf..."

"Someone walked in here and did not come out."

"What? I'm sure there must be a mistake."

"Is there a back door to this closet?"

"You've seen the floorplans, Dr. Sutter. There is no back door here."

You just kissed me and now I'm Dr. Sutter. Rachel was too busy looking for the latch to say it out loud.

When she felt the button on the back of the next to top shelf, she pressed it without saying a word. The back of the closet swung away and revealed a flight of stairs leading to a basement that was not on the floorplan.

QUICK WRITING EXERCISE: CREATE A SCENE

Using the information above regarding scene building, try creating a draft of a scene from your Romance. Choose a starting point that captures your imagination; it need not be the first scene in the story. Because you're building the structure of your Romance as we go through these chapters, you will be able to fit your scene into the appropriate place in the story.

What is topmost in your mind? The main characters' first meeting? A scene from a character's backstory? Take twenty minutes and rough out a draft of a scene you have in mind.

You may find the method below very helpful in organizing scenes into chapters. Plus it gives you an excuse to play with multicolored file cards.

WRITING CRAFT: ORGANIZE YOUR SCENES

As you write more scenes, drawing from the list of potential conflicts you generated in a previous chapter, you may wonder how best to organize them. One classic method is to note a reminder about each scene in a chapter on a file card, and then lay the cards out on a table. Play with the cards, lining them up in different ways until you have an arrangement that makes sense.

Once you have that order, you can move scenes around in your manuscript by cutting and pasting. Then read through each chapter and write connecting language as needed so that the scenes flow from one to another.

CHAPTER 9
ACT TWO PART ONE — THE CONFLICT BUILDS

Act Two of a Romance is where the rubber meets the road. The main characters come fully into conflict and act out their ambivalence toward one another, alternately approaching and avoiding intimacy. Events in the external plot give the main characters reasons to come together and run away. As conflict rises and resolves, trust ebbs and flows. And the sidekick characters provide counsel, scold their main characters, and may have their own agendas.

Act Two will take up about half of your story, and we will break it down into Part One and Part Two. Each of those parts has a defined structure. Act Two Part One of the Romance is our focus in this chapter. It typically looks like this:

- Introduce a challenge from the external plot that puts A and B into conflict.
- Next, illustrate the better qualities of your two main characters and the reasons for the attraction between them.
- Then introduce a conflict between the main characters, which may be strictly interpersonal or may be catalyzed by an event in the external plot.

- Some conflicts come to a resolution (which may be transitory), while other conflicts remain.

This cycle can repeat several times in Act Two Part One, with the characters dancing toward each other and running away again. They can take turns chasing and running while romantic tension builds. Both characters will likely reveal their feelings to their respective sidekicks, and each sidekick will respond based on shared history with their main character. By the end of Act Two Part One, there is a False High or a False Low: Either it looks like the two main characters will commit, or it looks like the main characters will break off their attempts at a relationship. Either way, this moment will not last.

The end of Act Two Part One should be roughly the midpoint of your novel.

As an illustration, the diagram below shows a breakdown of Act Two Part One for *Vampires of a Certain Age*.

ACT TWO PART ONE SUMMARY: *VAMPIRES OF A CERTAIN AGE*

Step Within Act Two Part One	Content Suggestions	Steps for *Vampires of a Certain Age*
1. External Plot Challenge	Thrown together by circumstance, the main characters face a challenge that makes them adversaries.	The undercurrent of suspicion between Rachel and Marion deepens as both Rachel and her sidekick Luke discover irregularities at the blood bank and try to make sense of them.
2. Vision of Better Qualities	Yet they are drawn together by certain shared interests, qualities, values.	Marion wrestles with the fact that Rachel is the living image of her long-lost love. In truth, both women are engaged in protecting public health, and both recognize that in each other.
3. Sidekicks React, May Intercede	Sidekicks start to learn about the main characters' feelings and circumstances.	Amber realizes that her boss, Marion, is attracted to Rachel and warns her of the dangers. Luke asks his boss, Rachel, if she needs to step away from the inspection because of her feelings for Marion.
4. False High or False Low	Midway through the story, there is the appearance of a resolution (either positive or negative).	Marion and Rachel touch hands briefly. But Rachel believes that Marion is trying to manipulate her, and both women know they must keep their feelings in check.

WRITING EXERCISE: ACT TWO PART ONE SUMMARY.

Fill in the Act Two Part One breakdown for a favorite Romance novel, or a favorite Romance movie (*Something's Gotta Give* is a good Seasoned Romance example—or choose another from the Resource section at the end of Part One). For a downloadable copy you can fill in on your computer, please go to https://stellafosse.com/wsrdownload.

ACT TWO PART ONE SUMMARY FOR A FAVORITE SEASONED ROMANCE

Step Within Act Two Part One	Content Suggestions	Steps for a Favorite Romance
1. External Plot Challenge	Thrown together by circumstance, main characters face a challenge that makes them adversaries.	
2. Vision of Better Qualities	Yet they are drawn together by certain shared interests, qualities, values.	
3. Sidekicks React, May Intercede	Sidekicks start to learn about the main characters' feelings and circumstances.	
4. False High or False Low	Midway through the story, there is the appearance of a resolution (either positive or negative).	

Now do the same for your own Romance story. Remember you can change this later, but this first take will give you a starting point for your writing. For a downloadable copy you can fill in on your computer, please go to https://stellafosse.com/wsrdownload.

ACT TWO PART ONE SUMMARY FOR YOUR WELL-SEASONED ROMANCE

Step Within Act Two Part One	Content Suggestions	Steps for Your Well-Seasoned Romance
5. External Plot Challenge	Thrown together by circumstance, main characters face a challenge that makes them adversaries.	
6. Vision of Better Qualities	Yet they are drawn together by certain shared interests, qualities, values.	
7. Sidekicks React, May Intercede	Sidekicks start to learn about the main characters' feelings and circumstances.	
8. False High or False Low	Midway through the story, there is the appearance of a resolution (either positive or negative).	

Dialogue is essential to the give-and-take of Act Two. As you write your story, understanding the role of dialogue and how to put it together will be key. Let's explore that now.

WRITING CRAFT: THE FUNCTIONS OF DIALOGUE IN ROMANCE FICTION

The information in this section will help develop your dialogue craft. Bear these ideas in mind, but don't allow them to interfere with writing your first draft. Dialogue was made to be edited, later! Dialogue in fiction is not like real dialogue. No one in a novel says "Hey, could you pick up bread on the way home?" (Unless, say, it's a murder mystery and the character they're talking to is actually dead.) Trivial dialogue might show up in a first draft. But when you come back later to edit your novel, keep in mind that fictional dialogue always has a job to do (and ideally does more than one job at a time).

- Dialogue reveals Character.
- Dialogue moves the story forward.
- Dialogue provides information (without being heavy-handed).

Dialogue also operates on what *isn't* said. Consider the backhanded compliment, the measured silence. For example: Imagine three varied responses to the question: "Do you like my new blouse?" What message does each of them convey?

Dialogue also identifies characters. In your Romance novel, your characters are distinct from one another, and their speech should be as well. Their lines may sound similar in your first draft, but by your final draft, ideally each character's speech will reflect their background and personality. We will circle back to distinctive speech in Part Two on Editing. For now, remember, your first draft is play.

In this early scene from *Vampires of a Certain Age,* dialog at a blood bank holiday party lets us in on some of the challenges Marion faces as a vampire in the public eye. In addition, these brief exchanges reveal an ironic aspect of Marion's character: As a vampire of a certain age, she fears *not* growing older in appearance (versus the pressures on mortal Women of a Certain Age):

When the event was over, Marion shook the speaker's hand. "Thanks for your comments, Mark. We're so focused on the day-to-day. It's great to hear your broader perspective."

"Glad to be here, Marion. You're looking well. When was the last time we ran into each other? Four, five years ago? You look exactly the same."

Marion said goodnight and made a mental note to add more gray highlights to her hair. Trying to look older was a bother. She headed for the parking lot, where Amber caught up with her. "You didn't eat. Again. You just pushed the food around your plate."

"Hmm." Why was playing mortal so tiresome?

"Marion. Are you going to tell me what's going on? You aren't sick, are you?"

She smiled. "No. Never better."

"Well then what is it? Come over to my house and talk to me."

Marion gave in to the inevitable.

WRITING EXERCISES: THE CRAFT OF DIALOGUE

Try one or more of these exercises to develop your skills at writing dialogue.

1. Copy a passage of dialogue from a favorite story. Analyze how the author uses dialogue to establish the character (including showing the characters' goals, strengths and flaws); to move the story forward (which includes establishing conflicts); and to provide information and backstory.
2. Go to a café and write down or type what people say at nearby tables (This is a time-tested practice for writers honing their dialogue skills). How would those conversations work (or not) as fictional dialogue? Which lines tell you the most about the speaker? About the events happening in the lives of the people at the table? When you get home, underline passages that sound like one of your characters.

3. For twenty minutes, with no stopping or editing, write the first draft of a dialogue scene between one of your main characters and their sidekick. Have the main character tell the sidekick about something they are planning to do; then the sidekick expresses concern about the source of the main character's motivation, based on background history; and finally, the main character agrees to consider a different action.

The next chapter completes the recipe for Act Two, as the conflict between the main characters rises to a crisis.

CHAPTER 10
ACT TWO PART TWO — THE BIG BREAKUP

The drama boils over in the second half of Act Two.

Part Two of Act Two will take up roughly the third quarter of your story. In a Romance novel, Act Two Part Two has a defined structure that (naturally) centers on the relationship between the two main characters.

- The characters' inner conflicts lead them to rising fears about each other and the relationship, with little to no recognition of their own inner wounds.
- Their worst fears are realized when one character believes the other has betrayed them.

By the end of Act Two Part Two, the characters have broken off their relationship and believe the break is permanent.

That breakup sets us up for Act Three, the resolution of the story, which we'll analyze in the next chapter.

Let's start with an example: a plot breakdown for the second half of Act Two in *Vampires of a Certain Age* that shows the rising tension until the supposed betrayal ruptures even the professional relationship between the two main characters.

95

Step Within Act Two Part Two	Content Suggestions	Act Two Part Two from *Vampires of a Certain Age*
1. Inner Conflicts lead to Rising Fears	Reveal each character's own traits that further complicate the relationship.	Even as the inspectors find more evidence pointing to major wrongdoing at the blood bank, Luke sees Amber, his love interest and Marion's sidekick, kissing another man—cementing his suspicion that Amber is leading him on—and confirming Rachel's suspicions about Marion as well.
2. Betrayal	The fulfillment of all the misgivings these characters have had about one another.	Rachel and Luke separately discover the hidden basement, from which they each believe Marion and Amber are selling infected blood.
3. Breaking off the relationship	There is still attraction but at this point, the negatives win.	Rachel tries to call in law enforcement to arrest Marion. All that stops Rachel is her physical collapse from illness.

WRITING EXERCISE: ACT TWO PART TWO

Fill in the Act Two Part Two breakdown for a favorite Seasoned Romance story—either a novel or a movie. See the Resource section at the end of Part One for ideas. For a downloadable copy you can fill in on your computer, please go to https://stellafosse.com/wsrdownload.

Step Within Act Two Part Two	Content Suggestions	Act Two Part Two for a Favorite Romance
1. Inner Conflicts lead to Rising Fears	Reveal each character's own traits that further complicate the relationship.	
2. Betrayal	The fulfillment of all the misgivings these characters have had about one another.	
3. Breaking off the relationship	There is still attraction but at this point, the negatives win.	

Now fill in the steps for your own story.

WRITING EXERCISE: ACT TWO PART TWO

Breakdown for Your Well-Seasoned Romance

Step Within Act Two Part Two	Content Suggestions	Act Two Part Two for Your Well-Seasoned Romance
1. Inner Conflicts lead to Rising Fears	Reveal each character's own traits that further complicate the relationship.	
2. Betrayal	The fulfillment of all the misgivings these characters have had about one another.	
3. Breaking off the relationship	There is still attraction but at this point, the negatives win.	

As you structure your second act, continue writing scenes that flesh out the full picture of the novel you are creating.

QUICK WRITING EXERCISE:

Draft a scene for your own Act Two Part Two where a main character tells their sidekick about their attraction to the other main character. Write this scene for a point in the story when the other main character is in running away mode.

AND SO IT BEGINS: THE TRANSITION FROM WRITER TO AUTHOR

The transition from writer to author means thinking of your book as a product and your author persona as a brand.

But wait, you might think. *I'm still writing the first draft. Why talk about this now?*

It's true that much of the marketing effort for a book takes place after the book is finished (as described in Part Four). But a savvy writer begins to lay the foundation for successful marketing during the early stages of writing. The work you do right now to build your author platform will pay dividends down the line because you will already have credibility with potential readers. And connecting with readers now will inform your writing and editing as well.

So when should you begin marketing?

The day you write the first sentence of your novel.

AUTHOR'S CRAFT: MARKETING FOUNDATIONS

If you are writing your Romance for yourself and your circle of friends, then marketing won't be on your radar. But if you are thinking of publishing your Romance, your job as an author includes marketing as well as writing your book. This is true even for authors whose books are published by traditional publishers.

The transition from writer to author means embracing the fact that your book is a product. It's your creation, yes; and people love to talk about their Book Babies. But your book is not your baby—it's your business. And your business begins with knowing yourself, your audience, and your book.

Who are You, as an Author?

When you consider what you have written over time, and what you want to write, what are your themes? What do you enjoy reading about and talking about? What, say, five subjects grab your attention and won't let go? These themes could relate to your career. If you've been in healthcare, your themes might relate to older women's health. If you've worked with computers, one of your themes might relate to the role of electronics in our lives. Your themes may relate to other passions. If you play cards, one of your themes might be socialization. Certainly the role of family in our lives could be a theme.

This personal inventory is important. It tells you how to build your online presence as an author. You may already have a social media presence in your personal life, and now you'll build a presence for your author persona. Consider creating author pages on the social media sites you frequent. Connect with other writers who think and write about similar themes. And it's not too early to construct a website for yourself as an author. The expectations of traditional publishers have changed in the last 25 years with the expansion of social media. Publishers now understand how much new authors can bring to the table in terms of social networking.

Who is Your Audience?

Romance readers read a lot of Romance novels. About half of all Romance readers read a Romance novel a week. These readers know the genre and know and enjoy its conventions. They expect the books they read that are labeled "Romance" to follow the format for a Romance novel—hence the focus on those conventions in this book.

Most Romance readers are women, and at last count their average age is 46. That means half of Romance readers are old enough to be the mothers of characters in their twenties. No wonder that as Romance readers age, many express frustration with the lack of main characters their own age. You're here to help!

How to reach that Seasoned Romance audience? By following their favorite authors online, by joining the groups they're part of on Facebook, and otherwise building your platform.

What is Your Platform?

Platform is your presence as an author. It is not only your online presence, but rather is a combination of your published writing, your relationships with readers and with other writers, and your ability to influence others through what you write. As your published writing grows and as you establish yourself through online and real life interactions with authors and readers, your influence will grow. So, where to start?

Community Building: Once you know what the themes will be for your writing career, find the folks who are doing what you'd like to do. Follow them and comment on their posts and blogs. And share posts of interest (with your comments) on your own social media pages. Be what Jane Friedman calls a good literary citizen (and if you aren't yet reading Jane Friedman, now is a good time to start). If you are a supportive presence on other authors' websites, they are more likely to follow and support you. That kind of community building can lead to greater things, like back cover endorsements from better known writers. But don't make it transactional; demonstrate your genuine interest in folks who play in the same sandbox.

Your Website: Whether you've been a pastry chef or a neurosurgeon, your extensive life experience gives you a leg up when designing your author website. Your approach to writing Romance will be distinct from everyone else's because of your unique life history and personality. Readers will enjoy reading your website for your bio, your FAQs, information about your writing process and what inspires you to write.

Include excerpts and information about your coming book, and update as you publish. Include an author headshot (professional if possible). Consider blogging about subjects of interest to you and tying them in with your writing. I have been blogging for five years and recently set up a Substack account where I re-share blogs I wrote five years ago, when I had few followers (Finding ways to re-share content to new audiences is one of the secrets of happiness).

Building a following is not instantaneous. But the best advice I got as a new author was this: When your blog only has five readers, blog as if you have ten thousand, and in time you will. And be sure to invite all readers to join your mailing list (check out the pop-up invitation at my website, www.stellafosse.com).

Of course, even while we are becoming authors, we are still first and foremost writers. Which brings us to the place where the twain shall meet.

Tell Us About Your Book…

Distilling the essence of your book into easily shareable phrases and sentences is an exercise that benefits you as a writer and you as an author/marketer. You will eventually share standard marketing language with potential agents and publishers, if you go the traditional route, or on the online sales pages for your book, if you go indie. By writing standard marketing language for your novel, you focus your efforts and give yourself a North Star to guide your writing.

Logline: This is the Romance novel's concept boiled down into one or two sentences (25 to 30 words). The basic pattern, which you can and should modify to suit your story, is something like this:

In a SETTING, two MAIN CHARACTERS have a CONFLICT caused by INCOMPATIBLE GOALS/VALUES and face EXTERNAL OBSTACLES as they try to FIND HAPPINESS.

Here is an example logline for *Vampires of a Certain Age*:

A medieval healer turned vampire finds her true calling in a 21st century blood bank, where she falls in love with the one person who can destroy her.

You will use your logline in a cover letter to an agent or publisher, on your book page in online stores, as well as in other marketing materials.

Tagline: This is a short, clever one-off with a ten word maximum. Use imagery to convey an expectation of what the book is about. The tagline is used by marketing people, on your book cover, posters, etc. It may also become the subtitle of your book, as in:

Vampires of a Certain Age: Five Hundred Years of Loving

Elevator Pitch: This is a quick, punchy set of statements designed to sell your book to a publisher or agent. It is immediately engaging, provides all relevant information, and opens the door to further discussion. Use it to explain your book clearly in a few words, including at the top of your back cover in a printed version. As you write your elevator pitch, keep in mind your target audience of Romance readers past midlife. Convey to them that this is a story about vivid characters with whom they can identify. The text of your pitch may include your logline. It should reference your prior work if any, and can cite comparable books. Here is an example from *Vampires of a Certain Age*:

Marion Chase is a healer in medieval Yorkshire. Falsely accused of witchcraft after falling in love with Cecily, she is ostracized by the Church and by her fellow villagers. Rescued by a vampire and now immortal, Marion joins a sanctuary in York dedicated to virtuous living for the undead. Centuries and many adventures later, Marion finds her true calling as president of a Chicago blood bank, providing ethically sourced blood to Midwestern vampires. There she falls in love with the one person who can destroy her: Rachel Sutter, an FDA agent and the living likeness of Marion's medieval lover.

Note that the Elevator Pitch does not include the end of the book. That's because for publicity purposes, you never want to tell your readers how the story ends—even though, as Romance readers, they expect a happy ending. If you pitch your book to agents and publishers, you'll present a full Synopsis including the ending, because these folks want to know exactly what to expect before they read your book and decide to represent you. But for now, while you're writing your book, a full Synopsis can be useful just for you, to help you focus. I wrote one for *Vampires of a Certain Age*. Even though I planned to indie publish and did not share it with publishers, the Synopsis gave me an endpoint to shoot for. Here are the concluding sentences that were not in the Elevator Pitch, above.

When Rachel discovers that Marion is illegally diverting blood, Marion confesses her reasons, and Rachel is certain the blood bank director is mad. But when Rachel succumbs to a terminal illness, Marion saves her and the two become lovers. Once a vampire, Rachel learns the importance of Marion's mission.

AUTHOR'S CRAFT: YOUR MARKETING FOUNDATIONS

Complete the worksheet below with your logline, tagline, and elevator pitch. Included first is an example with marketing messaging for *Vampires of a Certain Age*.

AUTHOR'S CRAFT: LOGLINE, TAGLINE, PITCH FOR *VAMPIRES OF A CERTAIN AGE*

Term	Definition	How to Write it	How Used	Example: *Vampires*
Logline	Book's concept boiled down into one or two sentences. About 25 to 30 words.	In a SETTING, two MAIN CHARACTERS have a CONFLICT caused by INCOMPATIBLE GOALS/VALUES and face EXTERNAL OBSTACLES as they try to FIND HAPPINESS.	The shortest possible pitch. In a cover letter to an agent or publisher. Quick answer to the question, "What's your book about?"	A medieval healer turned vampire finds her true calling in a 21st century blood bank, where she falls in love with the one person who can destroy her.
Tagline	Short, clever one-off. Ten word maximum.	Use imagery people know to convey an expectation of what the book is about.	Used by marketing on book cover, posters, etc.	Five hundred years of loving.
Elevator Pitch	A quick, punchy set of statements to sell your book to a publisher or agent. It is immediately engaging, provides all relevant information, communicates professionally and opens the door to further discussion.	What your book is about—minus the ending. Can Include: • What your bookAudience/genre • Logline • Prior work • Comparisons	Use it to explain your manuscript clearly in a brief period of time.	Marion Chase is a healer in medieval Yorkshire. Falsely accused of witchcraft after falling in love with Cecily, she is ostracized by the Church and by her fellow villagers. Rescued by a vampire and now immortal, Marion joins a sanctuary in York dedicated to virtuous living for the undead. Centuries and many adventures later, Marion finds her true calling as president of a Chicago blood bank, providing ethically sourced blood to Midwestern vampires. There she falls in love with the one person who can destroy her: Rachel Sutter, an FDA agent and the living likeness of Marion's medieval lover.

Now complete the version for your book. For a downloadable copy you can fill in on your computer, please go to https://stellafosse.com/wsrdownload.

AUTHOR'S CRAFT: LOGLINE, TAGLINE, PITCH FOR YOUR WELL-SEASONED ROMANCE

Term	Definition	How to Write it	How Used	Your Well-Seasoned Romance
Logline	Book's concept boiled down into one or two sentences. About 25 to 30 words.	In a SETTING, two MAIN CHARACTERS have a CONFLICT caused by INCOMPATIBLE GOALS/VALUES and face EXTERNAL OBSTACLES as they try to FIND HAPPINESS.	The shortest possible pitch. In a cover letter to an agent or publisher. Quick answer to the question, "What's your book about?"	
Tagline	Short, clever one-off. Ten word maximum.	Use imagery people know to convey an expectation of what the book is about.	Used by marketing on book cover, posters, etc.	
Elevator Pitch	A quick, punchy set of statements to sell your book to a publisher or agent. It is immediately engaging, provides all relevant information, communi-cates professionally and opens the door to further discussion.	What your book is about—minus the ending. Can Include: • Audience/ genre • Logline • Prior work • Comparisons	Use it to explain your manuscript clearly in a brief period of time.	

One Final Thought

As you develop your author persona, you might consider choosing a pen name. I've used two different pen names for very different types of writing, and have encountered these pluses and minuses. Only you can decide which way is best for you.

Reasons to Choose a Pen Name

- Separate Your Author Persona from Your Private Life: When I began writing sexy stories, I was still consulting

with biotechnology companies and did not want my real name associated with my books. I was also concerned about what my kids would think. I've retired now, and my kids are cool about my writing, but I'm established as Stella and will keep the name.
- Distance Yourself from Trolls: Fans can be inappropriate or downright nasty, especially for a woman writing sexy books.

Reasons to Use Your Real Name

- Credibility: When I set my first novel in a biotech startup, I drew from my professional background. But my pen name never joined a professional organization or managed a team of writers in a biotech company.
- Outreach: You know a lot of people by your real name. It's easier to tell them that you wrote a book, than to say, "This person who wrote a book is actually me."
- Simplicity: What to do when your circle of influencers become your friends? When do you break the news about your real name? And what if somebody writes a check to an imaginary entity? What a tangled web we weave when our fiction includes our own name.

These ideas and concepts will get you started on your transition from writer to author. For more detailed information on the strategy and logistics of marketing, please see Part Four of this book.

And now, let's continue writing your novel by analyzing the third act and preparing for your happy ending.

CHAPTER 11
ACT THREE — THE HAPPY ENDING

A Romance novel is built with a set of parameters that writers employ and readers expect. If we had to choose one defining trait above all others, it would be the happy ending. While these conventions have moderated somewhat from the big wedding, Happily Ever After scenario of yore, a Romance novel still requires at minimum a Happy For Now ending.

Of course, the end of a story is happy because of where you choose to end it. Romance novels about people in their twenties end before diapers and colic. Seasoned Romances end before the final trip to the memorial park. But the message of a Seasoned Romance is that, up to a point, the third act of our lives can be just as happy as the third act of a Romance novel. The kids are grown, and for those of us fortunate to have sufficient savings, our careers are winding down. What's left is the good stuff: dancing in the morning and sex in the afternoon.

Writing the third act of a Romance is fun because the characters get to enjoy themselves. Whether you are writing a "sweet" Romance (where the narrative stops at the bedroom door) or a "hot" Romance (in which we are privy to the innermost chamber), the resolution of your story is the culmination of the mutual seduction your main characters have carried on since first they laid eyes on one another in Act One.

But wait, you say: *Didn't they just break up at the end of Act Two?*

Yes, they most certainly did, and with seeming finality. But the first thing that your characters do in Act Three is wallow in regret, with the able assistance of their respective sidekicks, who will assure the main characters that they have made a terrible mistake and need to get over themselves. *It's time to heal that nasty Inner Wound*, the sidekicks will say. *Resolve the Inner Conflict that holds you back and keeps you miserable.* With their opposite main characters out of the picture, each main character will finally cop to their own contribution to the breakup.

Then you as the writer get to orchestrate the reunion of the main characters, give them a wonderful love scene, and (if you wish) share an Epilogue where your lovebirds show off their happy lives together in the future.

Act Three takes up about the last quarter of the story. In a Romance, Act Three has (you'll be shocked to learn) a defined structure. Here is a summary of the action in a typical Romance Act Three:

- Looking back on the breakup at the end of Act Two, the main characters reflect on what went wrong.
- They may each get advice and feedback from sidekick characters.
- Each main character takes responsibility for his/her failings and resolves to do better.
- External plot conflicts also resolve.
- The ending includes a love scene as the main characters begin their lives together.
- There may be an Epilogue where we see their lives unfold in the future (think of the last scene in the film *Something's Gotta Give,* when the main characters pass a grandbaby around at a family dinner).

Act Three concludes with a "Happily Ever After" or "Happy For Now" ending.

Here is an example: the outline of Act Three from my novel, *Vampires of a Certain Age*.

WRITING EXAMPLE: ACT THREE SUMMARY FOR *VAMPIRES OF A CERTAIN AGE*

Step Within Act Three	Content Suggestions	Act Three Summary for *Vampires of a Certain Age*
1. Introspection and desire to resolve differences	Each main character realizes they need to change; may have input from sidekick characters. Also – external conflicts resolved.	Marion transcends her need for secrecy and saves Rachel from her terminal illness. Rachel, now a vampire, has no choice but to overcome her innate skepticism.
2. Climax of story: Happy Ending	The main characters come together and pledge their love. Will likely include a love scene.	Marion and Rachel make love in the elegant home Marion inherited from a long-dead (mortal) spouse.
3. Epilogue: Glimpse of Happy Future	(Optional) – The characters are seen in the future, maintaining their passion for one another.	Marion and Rachel move to England, where Rachel is reunited with her expat children. The women visit Marion's medieval cottage before they found a scientific institute to study vampire biology.

Fill in the Act Three breakdown for a favorite Romance—either a movie or a novel. See the Conclusions & Resources at the end of Part One for suggestions.

For a downloadable copy you can fill in on your computer, please go to https://stellafosse.com/wsrdownload.

Step Within Act Three	Content Suggestions	Act Three Summary for a Favorite Romance
1. Introspection and desire to resolve differences	Each main character realizes they need to change; may have input from sidekick characters. Also – external conflicts resolved.	
2. Climax of story: Happy Ending	The main characters come together and pledge their love. Will likely include a love scene.	
3. Epilogue: Glimpse of Happy Future	(Optional) – The characters are seen in the future, maintaining their passion for one another.	

Now construct the Act Three outline for your own Seasoned Romance.

WRITING EXERCISE: ACT THREE SUMMARY FOR YOUR WELL-SEASONED ROMANCE

Step Within Act Three	Content Suggestions	Act Three Summary for Your Well-Seasoned Romance
1. Introspection and desire to resolve differences	Each main character realizes they need to change; may have input from sidekick characters. Also – external conflicts resolved.	
2. Climax of story: Happy Ending	The main characters come together and pledge their love. Will likely include a love scene.	
3. Epilogue: Glimpse of Happy Future	(Optional) – The characters are seen in the future, maintaining their passion for one another.	

Creating a Love Scene for Act Three

A Romance is about romance, which culminates in physical intimacy in Act Three. A Romance novel is an extended mutual seduction that develops from awareness of physical nearness all the way to a loving sex scene. The love scene you write for your happy ending will be the culmination of the sequence of escalating moves throughout your story.

Your love scene will draw on the work you've done to understand your characters, including the descriptions of each main character you wrote earlier. And because you know your characters well, *let them lead you through your love scene*. What would each of them be feeling in this moment? What do they most desire? Take the time to let your characters speak to you.

You can also draw on sensory details of your own experience. Think back on a big crush you had at some point in life, maybe as a teenager, maybe in your sixties. Remember how the other person appealed to you through the sound of their voice, through their facial expressions and particular details of their appearance. Let your characters feel that intensity of emotion and that specificity of connection.

Like any other scene in your story, your love scene:

- **Has a beginning, a middle, and an end**. How do your characters end up together in this moment? What changes for them because of this encounter?
- **Engages the senses of sight, smell, taste, sound, touch**. Do they share a glass of wine? What does the room look like? What do they feel when they finally touch one another's skin?
- **Can use humor to relieve the tension of the moment**. Maybe one of them is trying to be sophisticated and flubs it.
- **Leads to new issues or challenges for the characters**. While making love might solve some problems, it can create others. What are they still concerned about? Do they have new concerns?

Your love scene will be more powerful if you use sensual language and describe the experience from a main character's viewpoint. The characters' emotional experience is more important in

Romance than the intersection of body parts. The goal of a Romance story is to lead to a happy ending, and sex is only one aspect of portraying a loving connection between the characters.

How to Get Past Embarrassment about Writing a Sex Scene

If you sat down and described the mug from which you drank your tea this morning (its heft, the way it reflects light, the aroma of your half-consumed drink, plus the sensation of warm liquid making its way down your esophagus), your writing would have terrific sensual content. And there is no bright line between the sensual and the erotic.

Not to downplay the challenges of writing overtly about sex. Writers often have a hard time writing sex scenes. They become embarrassed, or don't know how to approach the writing, how explicit to make it, or what terms to use for parts of the human body. It's a throwback to how they may have felt about writing in general, earlier in their experience. It is writer's block all over again. And there are tools to help both novice and veteran writers deal with what we might call "sex block."

In previous chapters we have considered ways to encourage your Inner Critic to step aside, and this is especially important while writing a sex scene. It is what it is, that sex scene draft. It may be good, it may be terrible, and so what? If you don't write it, you can't edit it.

Just as important, find a way to play while you write your first draft. This is true whenever we write but especially when sexy material feels scary. Pretend you are a Martian narrating her first glimpse of human sex. Or pretend you are a piece of lint in one of the participant's belly buttons and tell the story from that angle. Pretend you are a neighbor trying in vain to ignore the sounds coming through your apartment wall. Anything that gives you a new, offbeat viewpoint will bring down the tension.

Once you have a draft scene, set it aside for a few days or weeks, long enough to feel less attached. Taking space from your draft scene reminds you there is more going on in your life (and in your novel) than your first try writing about sex.

Come back to your scene refreshed. When you take out your draft, read it aloud from a playful stance. Be a private investigator, reading to find evidence. Or be the Martian's significant other, who suspects that their partner prefers human sex to the Martian variety. Pretend you have synesthesia (a sensory confusion that allows people to see sounds and smell colors) and add the most outrageous sensory details you can think of. And don't delete anything from your draft until after you take it to that next level of outrageousness.

WRITING CRAFT: NINE STEPS TO WRITE A SEASONED SEX SCENE

At their best, sex and writing have a lot in common: two forms of play that engage us creatively with others. Both make us vulnerable. And there is no subject we can write about that makes us more vulnerable than sex—even more so for older women writing about sex in a youth-obsessed culture. Kudos to you for engaging in this fun revolution! Here are ideas to get you started writing fictional intimacy.

1. Let it Be What it Is.

Writing about sex can be tough because it feels personal, and in a way, it is. But remember, you're not having sex—your characters are.

So, where to start? Begin at the beginning. Your characters kiss, and someone takes off one item of clothing. Then just imagine: What if you had no scruples and no anxieties at all about your writing? What if you were absolutely free to write anything you wanted? Now write *that* version of the scene: brave and wild. You're not obligated to share your first draft with anyone. You can tone it down later for public consumption.

2. Why a Sex Scene at This Point in the Story?

A sex scene is not an isolated event. Like any other scene, an intimate encounter grows from the events in your story and the development arc of your characters. A sex scene exists to move your plot and your characters forward.

Be strategic. Plan where in the story your characters become intimate. The moment when everyone is ready at the same time, when barriers have broken down and trust is established, will likely not happen until late in the story. And consider how this scene changes things for your characters going forward.

3. Build in Vulnerability and Surprise.

When characters have sex, it's not just their bodies that are naked. We see their traits writ large. Consider how your characters' fears show up during sex—which may include discomfort about their present-day bodies. Or on the other hand, being sexual might help a character overcome a fear.

Characters can show new aspects in the bedroom. The shy one displays boldness we didn't expect; the mean one turns gentle in bed. Character development happens. Are your characters more emotional or more lustful than expected? Let them surprise you.

4. Engage Your Characters' Senses.

Write about all the senses, from the characters' viewpoint. Remember this is their scene, not yours. You might not mind Bach on the stereo during sex; your protagonist might hate it. Can she smell his aftershave? Does she like it? Is the washing machine running in the next room? Does he pay attention to the sound? Does her skin taste salty? Does the air feel chilly when she takes off her blouse? Does he notice the raised scar from her C-section? Bring your readers into the room through your characters' sensory experience.

5. Remember: A Sex Scene is about Emotion.

Based on all you know about your characters and your story, what do they feel from the start of the scene to the end? If you focus on their emotions, your characters' body parts will take care of themselves.

6. Choose a Point of View.

Initially you may want to go back-and-forth in this scene from one character's viewpoint to the other's. It's fine to write a first draft that "head hops," conveying what this experience looks like from each character's perspective. Later, when you edit the scene, you can choose to tell this scene from the mind of the character who makes the most sense (or perhaps from the one who has the most to lose). If you do change viewpoints, as I did in the example scene at the end of this chapter, manage the change carefully to keep your readers with you.

7. Just How Hot Is It? And that language thing...

Stories have all levels of "heat," from sweet to spicy, where *sweet* stops at the bedroom door and spicy has all the lust the author can muster. If you try writing *spicy* first, even if you move sweeter in your edits, you can decide if there are certain spicy details you want to keep.

Also bear in mind that it's quite possible to write a great sex scene about bad sex (and vice versa!). The job of the scene is to advance the story, not necessarily to bliss out your characters. If boring sex does a good job for your story, so be it. As Romance writers like to say, "your love scene is not about sex: It's about the relationship."

Not to worry in your first draft, but be aware when you edit that too much anatomical language (or euphemisms, or metaphors for body parts) can come across as clinical or even absurd. That's the stuff of the Bad Sex Fiction Awards (https://inews.co.uk/culture/

books/25-years-bad-sex-awards-106373), granted to some well-known authors who laid it on too thick.

8. Give Dialogue a Job.

People talk in the bedroom and characters do too. Not that bedroom dialogue in a Romance is the same as real speech, any more than realistic conversation of the "your shoelace is untied" variety belongs in the rest of your novel.

Depending on the mood of the scene, your characters may tease each other, compliment one another, set boundaries, give suggestions. You know what your characters are feeling during the encounter; what would they say (that will also advance the story)? How do they feel after they make love, and how would these characters express that? What has changed for them? The language your characters use should be true to each of them. That includes how they talk about sex.

9. Make It Real for Older Characters.

When writing about older characters, don't be afraid to mention how their bodies look and function now. But don't belabor it either. Just as in life, the reasons characters are attracted to one another relate to much more than their looks.

Include lube and toys in sexy ways. Read senior sex educator Joan Price (e.g., *Naked at Our Age*) and consider fun ways olders are likely to have sex, such as standing up (you don't need to point out it increases blood flow to the gonads). They can meet in bed in the middle of the afternoon (If they're retired, why not?). And sex after dinner means digestion competes for blood flow. In one of my favorite sex scenes to write, an older couple leaned against a dishwasher mid-cycle as it vibrated away (that's in *The Erotic Pandemic Collection*, if you're interested).

Consider how your characters feel about their bodies. Maybe a character is self-conscious but once turned on is focused on sensation, not appearance. As the scene progresses, feelings can change, lending depth to your characters and potentially changing their self-image.

Should your love scene be funny? If you'd like, but not at your characters' expense. Too much is written that makes fun of older bodies. The world doesn't need more of that.

Below are two writing exercises for your first draft love scene, using very different approaches. Try one or both.

WRITING EXERCISE NUMBER ONE: LOVE SCENE Q&A

Answer these questions about your romance scene:

- **Where does it happen?** Describe the setting, including details like the color of the room, the time of day, ambient sounds, the sensation of the bed covers. Is the room cool or warm? Bright or dim? Did someone build a fire in the fireplace?
- **What is each of your characters feeling** at the beginning of the scene? What are they noticing about each other's voices, hands, aroma? Is one of them more nervous than the other?
- **Who makes the first move?** Why?
- **What is each character feeling** about his or her own body? Are they self-conscious? About what, exactly?
- **For each character,** what feels important to say to the other in this moment? How does dialog alternate with touching?
- **Once they touch,** what else is going on? Do they make eye contact? Is one of them more eager, encouraging the other to make love?
- **What kinds of conflict could arise for these two characters in this moment?**

- **What do they say to each other** at the end of the scene?

Now use your answers to these questions as the starting point for the first draft of your love scene. Take all the time you need; write this first draft without stopping or editing.

WRITING EXERCISE NUMBER TWO: A MEMOIR-BASED APPROACH

Find a time and place where you won't be interrupted and open a new document on your computer. Consider a particular sexy time that was important in your life. Answer whichever of these questions appeals to you, quickly, without self-censorship or judgment:

- **What was the setting like?** Were you in a room, in a car? What did the place look like, smell like? What time of day was it? How much light was in the room? Did it feel safe and private, or open and risky?
- **Who was with you?** What did you love about the way he or she looked in that moment? What about the sound of their voice? What did they say? Did they initiate intimacy or did you? Were they hesitant, insistent, nervous?
- **What about you?** At the beginning were you excited, afraid, repulsed? How did you feel about your own body in that moment? How did you feel about their body? What did you experience through scents, sounds, sight? Did you fully consent to this event?
- **What was happening in your relationship with this person?** Why was this particular encounter important in the relationship? Was it the first time you were intimate or the thousandth?
- **What did each of you say?** What were you thinking? Were there moments that were incongruous, or even humorous? You can write this scene as a continuous narrative, or write out of sequence, as you wish.

- **Describe how you touched each other**. Write freely. Use whatever words you want. What sensations did you experience? Were these sensations new or familiar, with this person or another?
- **Write about how this encounter changed your relationship** with the other person.
- **How did this incident change you**, change how you viewed the other person, change how you saw yourself? How did you view it at the time, and how do you see it now? If this event was in any way difficult or traumatic, how did you deal with that?
- **What did you discover about your own sexuality?** Did the incident take you to new highs? Was it more exciting than you expected, or more tender? Did you feel happy? Fulfilled? Or sad that it came to an end?

Write all of this rapidly, and if your Inner Critic speaks up, let them know they will have a turn when you edit. And give this writing the time it deserves. You may choose to come back to it over the course of several days, answering different questions each day. Each time you write about these questions, keep the pen moving or your fingers moving on the keyboard. Don't look back, don't begin to edit, until you have said everything you want to say.

Whether or not the memoir-based sex scene works in your current story, hang onto it! After editing, it could be the seed for a future story—or a version of it may turn out to be just what you need in your Well-Seasoned Romance.

EXAMPLE: EXCERPT FROM A LOVE SCENE IN *VAMPIRES OF A CERTAIN AGE.*

Shoes, hose, suit jacket, skirt, all were cast aside. Hands were everywhere: caressing breasts, touching shoulders, massaging buttocks. Rachel's hands slid behind Marion's head and pulled her close. She found Marion's lips with her own, lips that tasted of time, the spices of long ago, the herbs in the garden of her burnt English cottage. Rachel could sense the remnants of iron on Marion's tongue, the errant proteins of expired blood. The taste thrilled her as if the blood were Marion's own.

Marion slipped her hand between Rachel's legs and her hand was cool as stone, cool as a spring breeze across the Yorkshire hills. Marion breathed softly into Rachel's ear as her hand glided up the sensitive skin at the inside of Rachel's thigh.

Rachel thrilled at the heightened sense of touch she experienced in Marion's arms. "Kiss me again. Please. Give me your tongue." With a low murmur, Marion did as she was asked.

Still kissing, the two made their way to Marion's bed, which was large and inviting, a slightly darker peach than the walls, with a generous silken canopy. Lying on it, Rachel felt as if she were floating in space. Marion's body was strong and soft, new and somehow familiar. Her fingers teased Rachel's nipples while her lips kissed Rachel's neck and gave her the tiniest of bites, a reminder of their exchange of blood just two days before. Rachel could not consciously remember that moment, yet some part of her thrilled at the reminder. She wanted to touch Marion too, but the sensations Marion gave her were so overwhelming that all she could do was moan through her kisses.

For Marion, stroking Rachel's body brought back memories of lying in a spring meadow with Cecily. Rachel's skin, the sounds Rachel made in desire, the way she held her limbs when excited, her wide-eyed gaze, all echoed that ecstatic time, and yet Rachel was new and fresh and in this present moment.

Later, as she lay in Marion's arms and played with a lock of her hair, Rachel said, "I thought we were going to wait a while."

Marion smiled. "I did too. After all, we have plenty of time. Then suddenly I was finished waiting. How about you?"

Rachel kissed her cheek. "Yes, I was ready, and I'm glad you were too."

Marion turned out the light, but with their heightened senses, they could clearly see one another's bodies—their lovely immortal bodies. And in Rachel's case, the body that was supposed to be in a sealed coffin at the funeral home, awaiting burial. But no truly dead body ever experienced what Rachel felt that night in Marion's arms.

If all writing is erotic writing, it is equally true that erotic writing is just writing. We can play with it, we can share it or keep it to ourselves, we can leave it as is or polish it. We own it and we don't need to be scared of it.

I suspect that all words are incantations, are forms of magic. And words about sex may be the most magical of all.

You now have the tools to plot your complete Well-Seasoned Romance. With that plot outline in hand, as well as your character arcs and the craft tools we have discussed, you are set to finish the first draft of your novel. Additional resources to support you on this journey are below, followed by Part Two on editing your draft and creating a final manuscript.

Congratulations! You are on your way!

PART ONE: CONCLUSION & RESOURCES

Part One analyzed what makes a romance a Romance and gave you the tools to create the premise, characters and plot that will bring your story alive. We also looked at craft elements including dialogue, setting, and more. If you've completed a first draft, congratulations! If not, please continue to write scenes for your Romance. Try the file card method at the end of Chapter Eight to arrange each chapter in the optimal order.

And before you move on to Part Two (Editing), please get a start on your platform and marketing foundation. See the "Author's Craft: Marketing Foundation" section in Chapter Ten. Along with your writing, this foundation is an essential part of your transition from writer to author.

Below are resources that you can use for inspiration as you complete the first draft of your Well-Seasoned Romance and build your author platform.

Onward!

RESOURCES FOR PART ONE:

Seasoned Romance Novels:

Here is a selection of Well-Seasoned Romance Novels. Find more by searching for "Seasoned Romance" or "Later in Life Romance" at your favorite online store.

Note the variety of publishers for these books: some traditional, some indie. You will find much more about publishing choices in Part Three of this book.

- Noelle Adams: *Late Fall*. Brain Mill Press, 2016.
- Sandra Antonelli: *At Your Service*. Sandra Barletta, 2019.
- Karen Booth: *Gray Hair Don't Care*. Amazon Digital Services, 2014.
- Stella Fosse: *Vampires of a Certain Age,* Baubo Books, 2023.
- Jasmine Guillory: *Royal Holiday*. Berkley, 2019.
- Eva Leigh: *Waiting for a Scot Like You*. Avon, 2021.
- Courtney Milan: *Mrs. Martin's Incomparable Adventure*. Courtney Milan, 2019.
- Natasha Moore: *Rescue Me*. CreateSpace Independent Publishing Platform, 2016.
- Nora Roberts: *Black Rose*. Berkley, 2005.
- Nan Reinhart: *Sex and the Widow Miles*. Fine Wine Romance, 2013.
- Helen Simonson: *Major Pettigrew's Last Stand*. Random House, 2010.
- Ceillie Simkiss *Second Wind*. Foxglove Fiction, 2019.
- Lynne M. Spreen: *Starting Over in Sedona*. Silver Life Press, 2022.
- Jeannette Winters: *Perfectly Seasoned*. Jeannette Winters Press, 2022.

Seasoned Romance Movies:

- *Elsa & Fred.*
- *Finding Your Feet.*
- *Hampstead.*
- *How Stella Got Her Groove Back.*
- *Last Chance Harvey.*
- *Letters to Juliet.*
- *Our Souls at Night.*
- *Queen Bees.*
- *Senior Moment.*
- *Something's Gotta Give.*
- *Supernova.*

Writing Craft Resources:

So many great ones! Here are three.

Jessica Brody. *Save the Cat! Writes a Novel.* Ten Speed Press, 2018.

Anne Lamott. *Bird by Bird: Some Instructions on Writing and Life.* Vintage, 1995.

Priscilla Long. *The Writer's Portable Mentor: A Guide to Art, Craft and the Writing Life.* University of New Mexico Press, 2010.

Marketing Foundations for Authors:

Mandi Lynn: *Grow Your Author Platform.* Stone Ridge Books, 2019. (Mandi also has an informative YouTube series)

Scholarly Dissertation on Seasoned Romance:

Sandra Antonelli (nee Sandra A. Barletta) Ph.D. Dissertation. *Cougars, Grannies, Evil Stepmothers, and Menopausal Hot Flashers: Roles, Representations of Age, and the Non-traditional Romance Heroine* (Exegesis). 2014.

On the Evolution of Older Women Characters in Fiction:

Ruth O. Saxton. *The Book of Old Ladies: Celebrating Women of a Certain Age in Fiction.* She Writes Press, 2020.

On Creativity in Later Life:

Julia Cameron. *It's Never Too Late to Begin Again: Discovering Creativity and Meaning at Midlife and Beyond.* TarcherPerigee, 2016.

Stella Fosse. *Aphrodite's Pen: The Power of Writing Erotica after Midlife.* North Atlantic Press, 2019.

PART TWO: EDIT YOUR WELL-SEASONED ROMANCE

CHAPTER 12
EDITING OVERVIEW

If you're anything like me, you enjoy the freewheeling process of writing a first draft but dread editing. I used to think of editing as pedantic and boring. In those days, unfinished first drafts clogged my hard drive.

To move novels from my computer to readers' bookshelves, I needed to bring the creative spirit into the editing process. I introduced several rounds of creative editing (before the proofreading stage, where my Inner Critic gets free rein). By the end of the process, my drafts were coherent and compelling—and yours will be too.

The whole thing is laid out in the chapters ahead. We'll start at the most creative, big-picture stage: developmental editing. You will learn imaginative ways to expand on the best things about your manuscript. In the following chapter, you'll carve away the parts of your manuscript that detract from your story, all the way down to line editing. In the final chapter, you'll learn where to focus your proofreading efforts and enlist the aid of your Inner Critic, who has been chomping at the bit all along.

But first, it's time to do nothing.

CHAPTER 13
THE COCOON PHASE

Imagine the inside of a cocoon. Do you picture a little caterpillar, all bundled up in a fuzzy coating?

Well, no, that's not what's really going on. The inside of a cocoon is basically goo. The caterpillar breaks down into mush and then is totally reconfigured as the butterfly.

Something like that happens when you set aside your first draft. The draft itself doesn't change while it sits there, but you do. That transformation we've talked about, from writer to author, happens in your brain while your manuscript is dormant. That's when your draft metamorphoses from your precious one into a product to sell.

How long should the draft incubate? Some of mine have been sitting for years, and that's not a developmental stage, that's just avoidance. But if you let your work sit for a month (or even two), your brain detaches from your first draft. When you take it up again, you'll see your story with new eyes.

That means you will hear your draft differently when you read it out loud. That means you won't be as bothered by making changes. Your manuscript is no longer your baby. It's your adolescent. And it's time for your book to grow up.

And meanwhile, while your manuscript is safely tucked away in a drawer (or a computer file—which you have of course backed up), it's a great time to consider joining one or more organizations for Romance authors.

AUTHOR'S CRAFT: USEFUL ROMANCE WRITERS' ORGANIZATIONS

Romance Writers of America (RWA) has gone through some changes these last few years. Take a look and see if it suits you. And certainly look at the Facebook groups for Seasoned Romance Writers that are outgrowths of RWA. Some locations also have in-person meetups for Seasoned Romance Authors.

There is also an international group based in the UK: the Romance Novelist's Association (RNA)

https://en.wikipedia.org/wiki/Romantic_Novelists%27_Association#History

Join RNA as a new writer and when you are ready, you'll receive an evaluation of your full manuscript as part of your entry fee.

Your writing exercise for the cocoon stage? Go out into the sunshine. Have lunch with a friend. And if you absolutely need to write, circle back to your logline, tagline, and elevator pitch, and make them the best they can be. Or write a blog on a theme that aligns with your novel and publish it on your website. But don't forget to rest. Soon enough, it will be time for the next stage.

Onward!

CHAPTER 14
DEVELOPMENTAL EDITING

Now that you've had a break, let's look at what creative editing is all about.

Professional editors talk about three phases: **developmental editing, line editing, and proofreading**. You start with the big picture and work your way down to the fine points. It's especially easy to be creative during that first, big picture phase. There are several components to developmental editing, including creative expansion of your story and a deep dive into its organization.

Expanding Your Story

When you write a novel, you explain only part of the big universe that the story occupies in your mind. That's one reason why it is important to let the manuscript sit undisturbed before we edit. How long you wait can depend on many things, including other time commitments. The point is to *leave the story alone until you can look at it objectively*. That usually takes at least a few weeks. If you can leave the document for a month or more, that's even better.

Then when you read the story, you bring new eyes to it. Read each chapter out loud to yourself and underline your favorite lines and most engaging ideas. Then write new material that comes to mind while you are reading.

Ask yourself these questions:

- As a reader, what do I want to know that the draft story doesn't tell me?
- What is hinted at but not fully explained?
- What ideas were in my head when I wrote this draft that didn't make it onto the page? Which of those are worth exploring?
- What about the sensory experience of the characters? What else are they seeing, smelling, hearing, touching, that should be shared with the reader to make the story more vibrant?
- Will the reader understand why the characters are doing what they do in each scene? Is it important to hint at, or explain, their backstory and motivations?
- What images does my draft create in my mind as I read it? Which of these additional images do I want to share with the reader?
- Does the story need more dialogue? More description of characters or setting? More plot twists? More conflict between the main characters?

EDITING EXERCISE:

Make it Bigger. Choose a scene and read it aloud. Does it evoke ideas that you haven't yet captured in writing? Expand the scene to address what is missing from your draft. Then read it again and add anything else your reader needs to know.

Repeat this process, scene by scene, for each chapter in your story.

An Organizational Deep Dive

Another key aspect of developmental editing is optimizing the organization of your story. Although Romance is a structured genre, you will find room to change the organization of scenes and even entire chapters.

Here are questions to ask as you review your draft:

- **Did I "dump" backstory?** In a first draft, it's perfectly fine to insert big blocks of backstory just to get them on the page. Now that you are wearing your Editor hat, think about teasing your reader with backstory. What do you want to hint about, and where? When, if ever, do you want to fully reveal important aspects of your characters' histories? Also, do you have backstory in mind that you did not capture in your first draft (including backstory for sidekick characters)? Consider whether it would be useful, and if so, write it down. Where in your story would this new material have the most impact?
- **Are my scenes in the ideal order?** For recurring interactions, such as the conflicts between characters in Act Two, what would happen if you changed the order of the interactions? What order will best grab the reader's attention, and keep her wanting to read more? Can you see a better pattern that increases the stakes, scene by scene? See the exercise at the end of this chapter.
- **Does the mutual seduction of the main characters' romance proceed in the best possible way?** Is it a gradual progression, from eye contact all the way through to intimacy? Do you want to play with that step-by-step seduction and jump ahead at some point, to startle your characters (and your readers)? Do the characters misjudge how things are going and do too much, too soon, requiring both your characters and your readers to step back, almost to square one?

- **Is the story fully structured in the manner of the Romance genre, with a beginning, middle and end?** What about the structure of each chapter? Each scene within a chapter?

EDITING EXERCISE: PLAYING WITH STORY ORGANIZATION

Consider outlining your story using file cards. Do this for a single chapter or your entire draft novel. Move the cards around and ponder what impact different versions of organization would have for the reader's experience. Do you want to add flashbacks? Start chapters with action? End chapters with cliffhangers?

Decide on the best order for your story and write any transitional language needed for the new organization.

Below is a schematic of the layout of cards for a Romance novel. Use this rubric or create your own to capture the final arrangement of file cards on a page.

CHAPTER RUBRIC FOR YOUR WELL-SEASONED ROMANCE NOVEL

Act One	Act Two Part One	Act Two Part Two	Act Three
Introductions / Inciting Incident	External Plot Challenge	Rising Fears	Introspection and Desire to Resolve
Main Characters Meet	Vision of Better Qualities of Other Main Character	Betrayal	Resolution: Main Characters Pledge Love
Main Characters Thrown Together for Entire Story	False High or False Low	Breakup	Epilogue: Glimpse of Happy Future

CHAPTER 15
LINE EDITING

The Art of Creative Subtraction

In Chapter 12 you added imaginative new material to your draft. But creativity does not always involve adding more words. Subtraction can be creative too. Consider how a sculptor works, freeing an image from a block of marble. And now that you've expanded your draft through the developmental editing process, this is a great time to create by subtraction.

EDITING EXERCISE: CREATIVE SUBTRACTION

- First, save your expanded version in case you want material from it later.
- Save a duplicate version, where you can begin to carve away phrases or even whole paragraphs that are not essential.
- Re-read a chapter of your expanded work. Consider: What is really needed to develop characters and storyline? What is extra, that is not needed and could distract the reader?

Cut that extra material, but don't get rid of it. Move it to a separate "Out Takes" file.
- Don't be afraid to delete passages you enjoy if they don't move your story forward (Writers call this "killing your darlings." It's part of that transition we've talked about, from writer to author).
- Now re-read your sculpted chapter. If you have removed material that was extraneous, the chapter will read more forcefully and more cleanly than before.
- Double-check the material you deleted in its separate file. Is there material that would add to your story, perhaps in a different location?

Repeat this sculpting process for each of your chapters. When you have finished, re-read your manuscript, adding connective language where needed to bridge gaps created by the process of subtraction. Your new post-subtraction draft will be stronger and more compelling than before.

Editing for Language

Finding the right words and phrases is essential to provide your reader with a rich experience. In a Romance, choosing the right words about attraction, sensuality and physical intimacy is especially important.

The process of editing for language is called the *line edit*, and while it is somewhat creative, it also involves the kind of detailed work that your Inner Critic will love to assist with.

Areas of Focus in Your Line Editing Process

During the Line Edit, please read your work aloud again, this time listening for **sounds** as well as for meaning.

- Take it a chapter at a time.
- Mark phrases that either don't scan quite right or don't say exactly what you meant.
- Also consider **tone:** Is it consistent, or is it serious one minute, jovial the next? Are there places where the tone does not match the events in the story?

Be alert for ageist words and phrases. These are appropriate if a character is overcoming internal or external ageism, but don't leave them unchallenged.

Now modify the phrases you identified to say exactly what you mean, in a tone that is consistent with events in the chapter. Delete **extra words** as you go; many adjectives and adverbs are not needed and detract from the impact of the story.

Also look for **writing tics**. When we write, many of us tend to reuse certain words, sometimes in the same paragraph. These tics can be hard to spot. Ways to catch them include reading your manuscript aloud, asking someone else to read your work, or using a software program designed to detect repeated words. Once you have identified overused words, consult an online thesaurus and consider other choices.

Pay close attention to **dialogue** as you read your work aloud. Your characters may all sound alike in your first draft (and, no surprise, they may all sound like you). As you edit, consider what you know about each character: where they grew up, their education level, their career and other influences. Each of your characters should emerge from this round of edits with their own vocabulary, verbal style, and preference for idioms.

While all your scenes deserve this level of attention, editing your Act Three love scene will require particular concentration.

WRITER'S CRAFT: EDITING A LOVE SCENE

Start by finding a quiet place where you won't be disturbed as you read the scene aloud. Take your time. The strategies for editing other parts of your book apply here as well: deleting extra words, watching for word tics, ensuring that dialogue is unique for each character, and so on.

As you read your love scene, notice phrases that resonate with you and phrases that make you uncomfortable. Editing a love scene requires that you be intentional about the level of heat you want in your finished book. Older main characters can enjoy plenty of heat, if that is your goal. Shape the scene to be more or less explicit, choosing words that convey meaning without being jarring. Anatomical terms can stop readers in their tracks, while euphemisms may introduce unintended humor. Look back at effective intimate scenes in other authors' books for inspiration.

Your edited love scene should convey the trust the characters developed in each other that brought them to this moment in the story. At whatever level of heat you choose, the primary focus of the scene will be the emotional resolution.

Next Steps

If you participate in a writing group, be sure to involve them in this editing process. When you read a section of manuscript to your group, ask them for the kind of feedback you want. When we are writing a first draft, much of what we need from listeners is encouragement to keep going. But by this point you are looking for guidance. You might want the group to tell you what's missing: What additional information would help them follow the story? You might want to know where they got bored, or which phrases struck them as awkward. By letting the group know what you want *before* you read, you can elicit feedback that will power your editing process.

If you are not in a writing group, look for a group through your library or a local bookstore. You can also find a writing buddy who is in the midst of their own editing process and then trade chapters with them as you edit. See Chapter 1 for more about writing groups.

At this stage, if you have developed a following through your social media platform and mailing list, consider asking for feedback from your followers and your fellow writers online. Trying to decide between two possible plot twists? Considering adding a secondary story line? Weary of a character's name and want to change it? Run it by your crew and ask their opinion.

This stage of subtraction and line editing takes time, and it is time well spent. When you have completed the process with each chapter in your manuscript, a stronger story will emerge. And you will be ready for the last stage of editing: proofreading, where your long-suffering Inner Critic will fully come into their own.

CHAPTER 16
PROOFREADING

This part of the book is called "Creative Editing," but frankly, proofreading is not very creative. The good news: This last stage of editing is a fine time to let your Inner Critic be their persnickety self. Right now, that's just what you need.

We've all had the painful experience of reading a poorly proofread book. The resulting errors can be so distracting that many readers will stop after a few spelling or grammar glitches. Don't let that happen to your readers. As authors, we want to do our best work and keep our readers happy. Read your book for typos, swap with a reading buddy, even consider hiring a proofreader. Be alert for homonyms. Even reading aloud won't differentiate "break" from "brake".

The book you save may be your own.

Some Things to Look For While Proofing:

- **Point of View:** Is it consistent throughout? If the voice changes from first to third person, for example, does the change make sense in context? Is the shift at a point that is

less likely to confuse the reader, such as the beginning of a chapter?
- **Grammar:** Problems to look for include subject/verb agreement (I say, she says, etc.). Also look for sentences with missing verbs. Pronoun agreement and pronoun antecedents are also key.
- **Verb tenses:** If your narrative switches from past to present tense, does it make sense, or does tense need to be made consistent throughout?
- **Spelling:** Watch especially for the wrong homonym. Your spellchecker program may not catch "their" when you mean "there."
- **Punctuation:** It's so easy to leave off a period or use too many commas. Check every line of dialogue for matching open quotes and close quotes.
- **Capitalization:** Proper nouns, first word in a sentence—remember those rules from English class?
- **Repetitive word usage ("tics"):** Re-check for this. Get out your thesaurus and find alternatives in passages where the same word appears several times. This is one of many reasons why reading out loud is essential. When we read silently, these word tics don't stand out.

Proofreading Methods:

- Use a **style guide** for American English. The leading contenders are listed in the Resource guide at the end of Part Two.

- Send out review copies to Beta readers. These are readers who agree to give you feedback on the full manuscript. You might ask people in your writing group, fans of your blogs, or other friends who are writers to read a Beta draft for you in exchange for a free copy of the final published version. Five readers are likely enough so that you can see if there

are patterns in the responses. Being a Beta reader is a thoughtful thing to do for a writer, and be sure to thank those who participate. If you are looking for specific kinds of feedback, include a list of questions along with your draft. Give your readers a deadline for feedback (three weeks is plenty of time; be sure your readers understand you won't be able to use late feedback). Thank each reader as you receive their feedback. Evaluate the comments and incorporate those that are useful. And do include these readers in your Acknowledgments. When your book launches, send each Beta reader a free final copy, with thanks and a request to review your book on Amazon, Goodreads, BookBub, etc.
- **Swap drafts** with a writing buddy. Each of us has particular errors we tend to miss in our own writing, even after multiple readings. A fresh set of eyes is essential. If you happen to have friends who are professional proofreaders, be very nice to them.
- **Hire a proofreader**. Do this after you and your reading buddy have been though your document several times. Hiring a proofreader is a particularly good idea if you are planning to self-publish, because you won't have a publishing house editor at your disposal. When I was editing *Vampires of a Certain Age*, two professional proofreaders caught different errors, with less overlap than I expected.

> Pro Tip: Catching every error takes multiple readings! And multiple readers!

PART TWO: CONCLUSION & RESOURCES

In Part Two we have covered the stages of editing, from big picture down to the tiniest detail. Even when you think your manuscript is complete, it's quite possible that proofing errors still lurk. If you are publishing via the traditional route, your publisher will issue Advance Review Copies for reviewers that will say right on the cover that the final proofread is still to come. And if you are publishing indie, you can generate your own ARCs (We'll talk about how to use ARCs in Part Three).

You can read your ARC in parallel with reviewers and ask your friendly proofreader to do the same. It will be remarkable if not one single typo shows up.

And when that final proofread is done, congratulations! You've done what others only dream of doing: *You've written a book.*

It's time to publish.

Below are resources you can use during your editing process.

Romance Writers' Organizations

Romance Writers of America (RWA) — Has some chapters for Seasoned Romance writers, as well as a Seasoned Writers group on Facebook.

Romance Novelists' Association (RNA) — An international organization based in England. Offers a critique of first romance novels as part of the registration fee for new authors.

Resource Books on Editing

Susan Bell. *The Artful Edit: On the Practice of Editing Yourself.* W. W. Norton & Company, 2008.

Lynne Truss. *Eats, Shoots and Leaves: The Zero Tolerance Approach to Punctuation.* Avery, 2006.

Style Guides for Proofreading

The Elements of Style is the classic. *Time Magazine* calls it one of the 100 most influential books in the English language. It covers usage, composition, voice, spelling, and much more.

The Chicago Manual of Style is the standard in American book publishing. It covers not only the basics of writing and proofreading in American English, but also has resources for publishing and self-publishing.

Guide to Intimate Terminology for Love Scenes

Cara Bristol: *Naughty Words for Nice Writers*, Third Edition. Cara Bristol, January 2021.

PART THREE: PUBLISH YOUR WELL-SEASONED ROMANCE

CHAPTER 17
PUBLISHING OVERVIEW

That manuscript you've sweated over deserves the best publishing home you can provide. But what is the best home for your novel? How to decide among so many choices? And it's not just a choice among publishers. These days there are various paths to publication, some of which did not exist twenty years ago. Whether or not you have finished writing and editing, it's not too soon to consider your options. Here is a quick summary, and the chapters ahead will explore each route in depth.

- **Traditional publishing:** The publisher chooses which books to support, in many cases with recommendations from a literary agent. There is no upfront cost to the author. The publisher pays for editing, production, cover design, printing and marketing, and has the final say on all of these. The author may receive an advance against future royalties. The agent, if any, takes a percentage of both the advance and the royalties. The publisher retains certain rights to the book (which may include movie, audiobook, and international rights depending on your contract). The author retains the copyright and other rights they negotiate. The publication process can take up to two years (or more if you use an agent).

> PROS: Traditional Publishing is good for authors who want to sell through bookstores, and who do not want to share in the upfront cost of publishing their book. It is also good for authors who want an advance as part of their compensation.
>
> CONS: Traditional Publishing is not ideal for authors who want more creative control over their final product, or who want to keep a higher percentage of their revenues.

- **Hybrid publishing:** The hybrid publisher chooses which books to support. The author contracts with the publisher for the services they choose, which may include editing, production, and cover design. Marketing may be available through the hybrid publisher or an affiliate. The author pays upfront for these services and then receives a higher royalty than with a traditional publisher (There are no advances). The author retains more control over decisions such as cover design than with a traditional publisher. While publication time can be as short as 3-4 months, the popularity of some hybrid presses has pushed their launch dates out to as much as two years.

  > PROS: Hybrid publishing is good for authors who want more creative control but don't want to manage the entire publishing process. Depending on the hybrid press, this path may also be good for authors who want to publish quickly.

> CONS: Hybrid publishing is not ideal for authors who don't want to share in the upfront cost of publishing their book.

- **Indie publishing (also called Self-Publishing):** The author publishes the book and controls the editing process, production, cover selection, and marketing. The author may outsource some of these tasks by hiring an editor, a book producer, a cover designer, and/or a publicist. The author receives all revenues, but also pays the editing production and marketing costs. Once the book is finalized, publication time is much shorter; it can be as brief as 24 hours on Amazon. The author retains all rights to sell any format of the book in any country (unless she chooses Amazon's exclusivity program, Kindle Unlimited).

  > PROS: Indie publishing is good for authors who are comfortable running their own publishing and marketing process (contracting for services as needed). Indie publishing is good for authors who want to retain the highest percentage of revenues. It is also good for authors who want to publish quickly, and who have the funds to pay upfront for the services they need.

  > CONS: Indie publishing is not ideal for authors who want widespread bookstore distribution. It is also not ideal for authors who prefer others to manage their publication process.

Whichever route you choose will involve tradeoffs: more or less control over your product, shorter or faster time from manuscript to publication, and how much or little time you must devote to logistics and marketing. Bottom line: The more you do yourself, the bigger your piece of the pie. And keep in mind that you will learn a tremendous amount while publishing your first book. As a result, the pathway you choose for your second book may be different than for your first.

The following chapters delve into the nuts and bolts of each publishing model. But first, some background on how publishing has evolved.

Publishing has Changed Over Time

The publishing business is a moving target. The publishing industry of the twentieth century was certainly not its first incarnation. Oral storytelling predates any written stories, and the earliest books were copied by hand. Block printing by the page increased production, with authors paying those printers directly. The invention of moveable type in the 1400s and increasing literacy rates eventually led to the publishing industry as we knew it in the twentieth century.

The publishing business has continued to evolve in the twenty-first century. Many of the big publishers we remember from former decades are gone. There has been massive consolidation, due in part to the failure of traditional publishing to embrace the e-book in its early days. This failure created an opportunity for competition against the industry itself. Amazon Publishing, founded in 2009, became the publishing behemoth that now sells around two-thirds of all books purchased in the United States, including about 80% of e-book sales. And while one of the functions of the traditional publisher was to pay for large print runs, improvements in Print on Demand (POD), the process of printing each book as it is ordered, made that function less important. Ingram Spark, one of the leading POD producers, enables bookstores to order any book. And because of e-books and POD, no recently published book truly goes out of print. Together, Amazon and POD made self-publishing (also called indie publishing) accessible to writers everywhere.

The democratization of publishing gives voice to writers who might have encountered bias from agents and publishers, the traditional gatekeepers. In the past, traditional publishing favored white male authors, while critics looked down on the Romance genre. Indie publishing has no such barriers. And the proliferation of indie books by writers in marginalized communities spurred traditional publishing houses to focus on raising up diverse voices. All that is good news, but there are reasons why the picture is more complex.

- First, indie publishing has led to an explosion in the number of books on the market. By one estimate, there were about 500,000 book titles available in 1990 and there are 20 million titles available today. This enormous supply makes it difficult for any particular author or book to stand out (although there are great opportunities for an underserved niche like Well-Seasoned Romance—see Part Four for marketing ideas).
- Second, the number of bookstores in the United States has dropped by about 12% since 1997 due to competition from online sales. The brick-and-mortar bookstores that remain are under financial pressure and stock fewer books than they once did. And as the remaining stores struggle to compete with online purchases, they have a greater incentive to stock books from big publishing houses with big marketing budgets.
- Third, because there are fewer barriers to entry in indie, there is no one to stop a poorly written and badly edited book from going on the market. This makes it tough for other indie books—even great indie books—to gain a foothold.
- And fourth, the explosion of sales at Amazon has enabled the company to behave like a monopoly, cutting royalty rates and introducing new fees for authors (as well as for video artists and musicians). As you will see in the indie publishing chapter, Amazon is a relatively accessible way for new authors to publish. How attractive that avenue

remains may depend on whether antitrust lawsuits in the United States and Europe expand to include book sales.
- One trend to watch: More and more authors are selling books directly from their own websites and keeping nearly 100% of their e-book cover price, as compared with the current top Amazon royalty rate of 70% less a "delivery" fee (for lower priced books, the Amazon royalty rate is 35% as of this writing).

The industry continues to develop, and so will you. Which way you choose to publish will depend on what is important to you. I know writers who are so keen on a short timeline they would never consider anything but indie publishing. Other writers are intent on a wide distribution in physical bookstores, which typically requires a large traditional publisher (and representation by a literary agent). Some authors cherish the camaraderie found in certain hybrid publishing environments (such as SheWrites) and are undaunted by the fees involved. Each of these options has strengths and weaknesses, which we will detail in the chapters ahead. Given those many factors, writers may choose different publishing routes depending on the project.

The chart below compares finances and processes across the three main publishing models. Note the differences in creative control and timing, in addition to finances, across the three pathways.

AUTHOR'S CRAFT: SUMMARY OF THREE PUBLISHING MODELS

For a full discussion, see the following chapters on each of the three options.

	Traditional Publishers*	Hybrid Publishers	Indie (Self) Publishing
Financial Comparison			
Fees Charged	None.	Depending on publisher, may be $3000 to $25000	The author pays for services she outsources, which may include cover design, editing, production.
Typical Advance	Five figure (or higher) advances from the "Big Five" New York publishers. Four figure advances from midsize traditional publishers. No advance from small traditional publishers.	None	None
Typical Royalty Rate	Varies per contract and publisher, but can be (per Authors Guild): • For Hardcover: 10% of revenues • For Paperback: 8% of revenues • For eBooks: 25% of revenues • For audiobooks: 25% of revenues Note: Advance must be earned back before any royalties are paid. Contract may allow for reserve against returns.	25% to as much as 80% of revenues depending on contract and publisher	Royalties can be 35-70% for online stores, less delivery fees. The author receives almost 100% of revenues from books sold on her own website.

*If you engage an agent, the typical fee is 15% of author revenues (advances and royalties).

	Traditional Publishers	Hybrid Publishers	Indie (Self) Publishing
Process Comparison			
Creative Control	Author's control is limited.	Greater creative collaboration / control.	Full creative control.
Logistics	Publisher responsible for editing, ISBNs, book design, cover design, formatting, printing, distribution online and to bookstores.	Publisher responsible for editing, ISBNs, book design, cover design, formatting, printing, distribution online (depending on contract).	Author responsible for all logistics; depending on author skills and finances, may outsource certain tasks.
Marketing and Publicity	The publisher will take the lead and will expect full participation from the author. Publisher support may wane after the first three months.	Many hybrids do not promote or market but will refer to a publicist for additional fee.	Author fully responsible; may choose to hire a publicist and/or marketer.
Time to Launch	Up to two years; can be up to four years if author first presents to an agent.	Can be months (Some hybrids now so popular that timing approaches two years)	Can launch in days or weeks from manuscript completion (barring delays in outsourced services)

The next three chapters will delve into each publishing pathway in turn. But before moving on to those chapters, there are four topics that are important to know about, regardless of the route you ultimately choose.

- **Quotations:** If you quote another author, you will likely be responsible to obtain permission, even with a traditional publisher.
- **ISBNs:** International Standard Book Numbers are essential to the entire book industry.
- **Scams:** Publishing scams affect each publishing route, though the scams themselves may differ.
- **Contracts:** Publishing contracts are important to understand, and they differ depending on whether you work with a traditional publisher, a hybrid publisher, or with service providers as an indie author.

Keep these points in mind as you map out your publishing strategy.

Quoting Other Authors

Regardless of your publishing path it's important to avoid the potential for legal issues if you quote another author. After all, just as you own the words you write, so does every other author (and lyricist). Please note that I am not an attorney, and you should consult a literary attorney if you are planning to quote another writer. I only offer observations from the viewpoint of an author who has used quotations in my work. Please see the Resources at the end of Part Three for more about copyrights.

Publishing contracts typically require the author to obtain and pay for all necessary permissions. Here are a few points to keep in mind and to discuss with your literary attorney.

- **Public Domain:** Copyright exists to protect the words of writers like you and me. And the flip side is that copyright eventually expires to enable future writers to build on those creative works. The rules differ depending on when the work was published vis-à-vis enactment of various copyright laws. In the United States, creative products are typically protected for 95 years from publication (50 years if published under a pen name). After that, these works enter the public domain (For example, in 2024 *Lady Chatterley's Lover* entered the public domain and became eligible for quotation, adaptation and fan fiction). I'm not saying that quoting another author is always a bad idea. After all, I quoted these lines in *Vampires of a Certain Age*—written by Queen Elizabeth the First:

> I am and not,
> I freeze and yet am burned,
> Since from myself
> Another self I turned.

Sixteenth century author? Pretty safe to quote.

- **Fair Use:** Short quotations of works not in the public domain may potentially be quoted under the Fair Use provision of copyright law. This is a contentious area that has spawned many lawsuits. Authors of song lyrics have been especially successful at prosecuting these suits, even for brief quotations, because the percentage of the full lyric quoted is high compared to quoting the same number of words from a novel. Please consult a literary attorney if you are considering a Fair Use rationale to quote lyrics (or anything else) without the author's permission.
- **Obtaining Permissions:** If you decide to include a quotation that is copyright protected, contact the copyright owner to obtain permission. Even traditional publishers

typically require that the author—not the publisher—obtains (and pays for) permissions for quotations.

Bottom line: Is the quote, apt as it may be, worth the trouble and expense? Only you know for sure. But bear in mind that if you do use a quotation, paying for permission is less expensive than a copyright infringement lawsuit.

ISBN Basics

Take a book off your shelf, look at the back cover, and you will see a bar code called an International Standard Book Number, or ISBN. This number uniquely identifies a book and enables any bookstore, library, or individual to order it. If a traditional or hybrid publisher publishes your book, obtaining ISBNs for each of your formats will be part of their job. If you indie publish, you will purchase your own ISBNs. In the United States, a company called Bowker is the only original seller of ISBNs. If you buy an ISBN from another company, they will likely charge you a markup over the Bowker price, and the company that sold you the ISBN then actually owns the number.

Amazon, Barnes & Noble, and Ingram Spark can supply an identifying number if you self-publish, but the numbers are not accepted by all distributors. A Bowker ISBN is the gold standard.

If you indie publish your work, you may wish to purchase ISBNs in your own name or the name of an imprint you establish (my imprint, for example, is Baubo Books). Once you purchase a block of ISBNs, the imprint name you use cannot be changed.

Publishing Scams

As the number of new writers publishing books has skyrocketed, scams designed to take advantage of writers have proliferated. At every stage of the process, from editing to marketing, there are unqualified and unscrupulous people ready to take your money. Scammers exist in every publishing pathway. They include fake literary agents, fake editors, entire fake publishing companies, as well as scammers claiming to work for top New York publishers.

When someone approaches you with an opportunity, do your due diligence. Does their email address match who they claim to be? Is their offer in line with industry expectations, or is it too good to be true? Can you verify with other writers that their services are as represented? Are they asking for money, even though they claim to represent a traditional agent or publisher? If you call the company they claim to work for, can others vouch for them? Online resources such as Writers Beware and the Authors Guild have more information on literary scams (see the Resource guide at the end of Part Three).

In addition to outright scams, there are erstwhile publishing professionals who are simply ineffective. Anyone can call themselves a literary agent, for example, although some lack the skills and connections to be effective. And small presses can get bogged down and essentially stop doing the job, though writers' contracts may tie them to a dysfunctional company. Again, do your due diligence—and be mindful of risks when negotiating a publishing contract. Avail yourself of a literary attorney (or join the Authors Guild for access to a contract review).

Publishing Contracts

Unless you yourself are performing every function of a publisher, you will have agreements with others to help bring your manuscript to publication. When you publish your first book, you may be so excited that you're tempted to sign whatever is put in front of you (I know I was). Don't do it. Instead, read and understand what you are being asked to sign. Ask questions and negotiate. Review the information about contract provisions in the next three chapters, because contracts differ depending on route to publication. And find a good literary attorney.

Regardless of which path you take, be positive and professional in your dealings with agents, publishers and contractors. Being a good literary citizen means being an author others enjoy working with. Publishing a book is tremendously satisfying, and it's also a great learning experience. If you go on to publish several books, you are sure to learn more, and feel confident taking on more, with each new book. The publishing process is challenging regardless of your path, and it is worth the challenges. There is no feeling in the world like opening the box of your author copies and seeing your new book born into the world.

Next, more about your options to make that happen, beginning with traditional publishing.

CHAPTER 18
TRADITIONAL PUBLISHING — WITH OR WITHOUT AN AGENT

When you think about publishing a book, you may picture a big publisher that pays an advance, provides services such as editing and marketing without charging fees, and is able to place books in bookstores. You might even assume that you need an agent to find a traditional publisher (which actually depends on the publisher).

The traditional model does have advantages. First off, a traditional publisher, especially a large New York publisher, has access to bookstore distribution that other publishing routes cannot match. A large traditional publisher also has established relationships with reviewers and media that may be tough to crack on your own. And it's the only model with no upfront costs to you; in fact, you may get an advance. Be aware, though, that not all traditional publishers can do everything the Big Five publishers can do. On the other hand, many smaller publishers can be approached directly, without an agent.

The chart below describes some of the differences between the Big Five, midrange publishers, and small independent publishers. Of course, these are generalizations; for example, even the Big Five have some imprints that do not require an agent.

Comparison of Three Sizes of Traditional Publishers

Publishing Category	Examples	Where Located	Requires an Agent?	What These Publishers Do for You
Major Publishers ("The Big Five")	1. Penguin Random House 2. Simon & Schuster 3. HarperCollins 4. Macmillan 5. Hachette	New York City	Yes (Although some have no-agent imprints for Romance, such as Forever Yours, Avon Impulse, and Carina Press)	Advances may be as much as 5 or 6 figures. Editing, cover design, publishing logistics, access to leading reviewers, publicity, marketing, distribution to brick and mortar stores.
Midrange Publishers of Romance	Kensington Publishers Carina Press (an imprint of Harlequin) Sourcebooks Casablanca	Usually in major regional markets	Usually not, though some do require an agent	May give four figure advance. Provide editing, cover design, publishing logistics, limited publicity and marketing, distribution.
Small Publishers	Vinspire* City Owl Press Literary Wanderlust Sibylline Press**	All over the country	No	Some editing; cover design, publishing logistics, distribution. Publicity and marketing support may be limited.

*Vinspire is a woman-owned press that only accepts Romance novels with characters over 45.
**Sibylline is a woman-owned press that publishes "the brilliant work of women authors over 50." They consider themselves a traditional press, though authors contribute to marketing costs.

Knowing that there is great variety within traditional publishing, the next question is:

Do You Need an Agent? And Where Would You Find One?

A good literary agent can use their contacts to find you a publisher. They can represent you in negotiations for an advance and a contract. On the flip side, agents have their own submissions process which delays eventual publication, and they take a commission which is typically 10-15% of your royalties (and your advance, if any).

Whether you need an agent depends on which publishers you

target. If you have your heart set on a major New York publisher, then yes, you do need an agent (unless you submit to an imprint of a large publisher that takes Romance submissions without representation, such as Forever Yours or Avon Impulse). On the other hand, if you decide to work with a medium or small traditional publisher, chances are you can apply directly. To help you decide, let's talk about what an agent brings to the table—and how much they take off the table.

What Do Agents Do, Exactly?

A literary agent helps a writer get their book published. The value of an agent is based on their reputation with publishers as someone who pitches high-quality work. Agented work typically bypasses the "slush pile" where unsolicited manuscripts of unknown quality land. As a result, writers gain access to larger publishers who prefer to see only manuscripts that have gone through a pre-vetting process.

An agent works with the writer to ensure that the manuscript meets their standards. This involves an initial evaluation plus giving editorial feedback to the writer. This back-and-forth process between writer and agent can take up to two years before the agent shares the manuscript with publishers, adding to the length of time to launch.

Once the agent has successfully placed the manuscript, the agent interfaces between the writer and the publisher to negotiate the publishing contract, including the amount of the advance and the royalty percentage. After the contract is signed, the agent may be available to advocate for the writer if issues arise during editing and production.

These services can be valuable, but they come at a price in time as well as money. If you work directly with a publisher the process may take up to two years; working with an agent can add up to two more years upfront, before your manuscript hits a publisher's inbox.

Yes But—How Big is the Revenue Pie, Depending on Which Route You Take?

The major New York publishers may pay larger advances. They provide access to major reviewers, bigger publicity budgets and distribution to bookstores, all of which may increase sales. If you set your sights on one of those publishers, you will likely need an agent. Even with midsize publishers, an agent may increase author revenues by negotiating a higher advance and royalty percentage. As authors we can educate ourselves about the role of the agent and decide whether to act on our own behalf. If you decide you want an agent, there are several ways to find one.

AUTHOR'S CRAFT: HOW TO FIND POTENTIAL AGENTS

The tried-and-true method to find potential agents is to peruse the Acknowledgements sections of comparable books where authors thank their agents. Check your favorite Seasoned Romance novels as well as current top selling Later in Life Romances.

In person networking is another great way to meet agents and scope out their fit for you and your novel. Many writing conferences feature pitch sessions with agents. In addition, agents often lead workshops at major writing conferences where you can observe their style and ask questions. Another way to meet agents in the flesh is to volunteer for state or local writing organizations, where you can interact informally with agents who volunteer. Even if they are not right for your project, you can gain insights and referrals from the agents you meet.

Several online sites are designed for agents looking for particular types of projects. These include:

- **Manuscript Wishlist** (www.mswishlist.com).
- **Agent Query** (www.AgentQuery.com).
- **Query Tracker** (www.QueryTracker.com).
- **Duotrope** (www.Duotrope.com).

With the exception of Duotrope, which also functions as a publisher search tool, all these sites are free. Search for agents interested in Seasoned Romance, Later in Life Romance, books with older protagonists, and so on. Make a list of possible agents and take note of their submission guidelines. To reach out to agents, put together your Query Letter and Synopsis (see the Author's Craft section later in this chapter).

Be prepared for polite rejections or no reply at all. It's all part of the publishing game. When you do connect with an agent and they express interest, read about them on their own website and in any articles they have published. Ask questions that will help you understand what it would be like to work with them. For example, you might ask:

- How many Seasoned Romances have you placed, and with which publishers?
- Which Seasoned Romance authors do you represent?
- What challenges do you face when working with Seasoned Romance?
- What is your preferred communication style with your author clients?
- Describe your process representing an author in obtaining a publisher, negotiating a contract, and in the post-contract phase of publication.
- May I see a sample representation agreement?
- May I speak with some of your recent clients?

EXERCISE: ONLINE AGENT SEARCH

Do one or both of the following:

- Search the agent-finding websites above for agents interested in Seasoned Romance or Later in Life Romance.

- Check out free resources about agents on the Authors' Guild website.

While an agent can be useful, also consider what you would do yourself to save that 10-15% agent fee. Are you interested in approaching publishers directly? Would you be happy with a midsize or smaller publisher? If so, read on.

How to Find Potential Publishers

Whether you use an agent or not, some of the work of finding a publisher falls on you. The materials you would write to reach out to an agent can also be used to pitch publishers directly (see the Query Letter and Synopsis information below).

There are several ways to locate promising publishers without an agent. First, check out who publishes comparable books. You can find out by a quick look at the online pages for other Seasoned Romance novels.

Second, there is good, old-fashioned networking. Back in 2017 I attended a writing retreat in Northern California. At one session I sat next to a woman I had not met and mentioned that I was writing a book encouraging women after midlife to write erotica. "I work at North Atlantic Press," she said, "And we would like to publish a book like that." And they did. Although a nonfiction book typically requires a query letter and a book proposal, I wrote neither. In 2019, North Atlantic published my first book, *Aphrodite's Pen: The Power of Writing Erotica after Midlife*. While my publication story is not typical, it illustrates how powerful networking can be. Go to retreats and conferences, talk with publishers, volunteer for writing organizations, and become known in your local and statewide writing community. Build your network before you need it.

Third, there are several online sites and services you can use to find a publisher.

- **Duotrope** is a site where you input information about your book and the algorithm matches you with potential publishers from their list of over 7000 houses. There is a fee for this service (which is very small compared with an agent's percentage of advance and royalties). Included in that fee is a submissions tracker, which is especially helpful if you are submitting lots of short pieces and want alerts when it's time to ping the publishers.
- **Manuscript Wish List**: Editors at various publishing houses provide their contact information and tell exactly what types of books they want to see in their inboxes. Just a few of these editors say "agented only."
- **Writer's Market** and **Literary Marketplace**: These classic tools help writers get published and get paid for it. Used copies of the *Writer's Guide* are available online with significant markdowns.

Once you have a list of prospects it is time to show off your work. To do that, turn your writing skills to crafting the marketing tools below, which are designed just for agents and publishers. Check each agent's or publisher's guidelines to determine what they require. And follow their requirements to a "T."

AUTHOR'S CRAFT: QUERY LETTER AND SYNOPSIS

The agents and publishers you pitch will likely request a Query Letter and Synopsis.

Back in Chapter Ten you crafted three foundational marketing tools for your novel: the logline, tagline, and elevator pitch. Review these tools and revise them to reflect your completed novel. They will come in handy as you write the documents below.

Query Letter

When you reach out to agents and publishers, your query letter will demonstrate that:

- You have done your homework on this particular agent or publisher and can show that your manuscript is an excellent fit with their goals and interests.
- You are a competent writer. Show don't tell: Your query is well organized, crisp, and free of awkward sentences and grammatical errors.
- You are qualified to write and publish your book. For example, if your characters are scuba divers, your background as a scuba instructor is relevant.
- Your book is interesting and worth their time to consider.

All that within 300-500 words.

Sample Query Letter

Although I planned from the start to indie publish *Vampires of a Certain Age*, here is a sample query letter I might have used had I pitched to agents or publishers. As you'll see, I incorporated text from my logline, tagline and pitch.

Dear {Agent or Publisher Name}:

A medieval healer turned vampire finds her true calling in a 21st century blood bank, where she falls in love with the one person who can destroy her.

After centuries protecting her identity why does this savvy

woman lower her guard for her greatest adversary? My new Romance novel, *Vampires of a Certain Age,* tells all.

As a mortal in medieval Yorkshire, Marion Chase fell in love with her friend Cecily and was shunned by her fellow villagers. Marion took refuge in a forest cottage and became an herbal healer. When a mob arrived to burn her as a witch, Marion was rescued by a vampire and joined a Sisterhood in York dedicated to virtuous living for vampires. Threatened by Henry VIII's men, the Sisterhood disbanded. Marion became a battlefield nurse and emigrated to America during the Civil War.

In the 21st century Marion runs a Chicago blood bank with a hidden sideline: providing ethically sourced blood to Midwestern vampires. All goes well until Marion encounters the one person who can destroy her: Rachel Sutter, an FDA inspector who is the living likeness of Marion's medieval lover.

When Rachel discovers that Marion is illegally diverting blood, Marion confesses her reasons. Rachel is certain the blood bank director is mad. Then Rachel falls ill, and the question becomes: Is any illness terminal if your love interest is a vampire?

My background is well suited to a book about blood. During my thirty-year career as a technical writer in the biotechnology industry, I worked with blood banks and FDA reviewers on approvals for new biological products. In my afterlife as a full-time writer and novelist, I draw on that background to create imaginative works based in science. I am the author of three previous books: *Aphrodite's Pen: The Power of Writing Erotica after Midlife* (North Atlantic Books, 2019); *The Erotic Pandemic Ball* (Baubo Books, 2020); and *Brilliant Charming Bastard* (Baubo Books, 2021).

Vampires of a Certain Age highlights key supporting characters who clamor for their own novels in the forthcoming Matriarchal Vampire Series. Planned future titles include:

The Vampire Vivienne — The vampire who saved Marion from the mob becomes a cross-dressing swordswoman;

Sybil the Barber Surgeon — One of Marion's companions from York learns a trade that provides her with plenty of sustenance; and

Kate's Jewels — Another of the Sisters becomes a Madam in Paris and then a philanthropist for women's causes.

Attached please find a full synopsis of *Vampires of a Certain Age* along with the first chapter. Thank you for your consideration, and I look forward to hearing from you.

Sincerely,
    Stella Fosse

EXERCISE: WRITE A QUERY LETTER

Using the bullet points listed under "Query Letter," above, write a template query letter for your novel that you can personalize to match the interests of particular agents and publishers.

EXERCISE: WRITE A SYNOPSIS

In Chapter Ten, you constructed a description of your book called an Elevator Pitch that excludes the ending of the story because it is designed to market to readers. You may also have written a full Synopsis, including the end of your story. If not, see the example Synopsis for *Vampires of a Certain Age* in Chapter Ten and write your full Synopsis now. The Synopsis will only be used to market your book to agents and publishers who need to know how your story ends for their selection process.

Once You Find a Publisher...

The process of finding a publisher takes time and energy, whether or not you work with a literary agent. You'll submit materials according to their guidelines, then track your submissions and reach out respectfully if they take longer to respond than their websites suggest. If you approach publishers directly, these are likely to be small- or medium-sized houses which vary in speed and quality. Smaller presses typically have smaller marketing support as well. Before you choose a publisher, ask lots of questions and talk with authors who have recently used their services. Once you have chosen a publisher, it is time to negotiate a contract.

About Publishing Contracts

> Disclaimer: I am not an attorney and the information below is not legal advice. I am only sharing what I wish I had known at the outset of my writing career. Please consult a literary attorney before signing a publishing contract.

A key step in publishing your book is negotiating and signing a contract with a publisher. Your contract spells out what your publisher expects from you as a writer, and in return, the support and payment you can expect before and after your book launches. A literary attorney or agent is your essential partner in crafting a fair contract that protects your rights. One cost-effective way to engage an attorney is to join the Authors Guild and use their contract review service. The Authors Guild also posts a template contract on their website with terms favorable to writers. You can download and study their template even if you are not a member of the Guild.

When you receive a draft contract from a publisher, consider it their wish list. Compare it with the Authors Guild template to learn how the publisher's contract differs in ways that benefit the publisher. Contract negotiation may well be outside your area of expertise—it's certainly outside mine. But to be an informed partner to your contract attorney or agent, it pays to learn some of the basics.

Main Contract Provisions and Negotiating Points

Here are major provisions you will see in a draft contract from your potential publisher, and perspectives you may find useful as an author.

Copyright: The copyright for your book automatically belongs to you. Some publishers ask writers to assign the copyright to them. However, the Authors Guild recommends you retain your copyright. They also recommend you negotiate to require the publisher to register your copyright with the United States Patent and Trademark Office within three months of publication, to protect your right to sue infringers for money damages.

Other Rights: The first draft contract you receive from a publisher may ask you for rights to all formats in all markets around the world. Those may include:

- **Primary Rights:** Print, electronic, and audio formats.
- **Subsidiary Rights:** Movie, television, theater, video games.
- **Territorial Rights:** All countries on all continents in all languages.

It's rare for a publisher to use all these rights. Clarify the publisher's capabilities and actual plans in a frank discussion. For example, ask: *Are they really planning an audio version? What are their firm plans for translation, and into which languages have they translated similar titles in the past? Are they actually planning to pitch this property to movie producers?* Your final contract should only assign to the publisher those rights they intend to exercise.

Plus, your contract should contain a Reversion of Rights clause for those rights the publisher does not exercise.

Reversion of Rights (from the publisher back to you): Your contract should make clear that the rights you assign to your publisher will come back to you under certain circumstances.

- **You should regain all rights if your publisher does not publish your book within an agreed time.** Ask your publisher how long after the manuscript is finalized they expect to publish your book. Your contract should state that if your book does not launch within the agreed time, all publication rights come back to you. This protects you from situations where a book languishes with an editor and fails to progress to publication.

- **You should also regain rights that your publisher owns but does not use.** The publisher may fail to create versions for which they negotiated rights (e.g., an audio version, or a Spanish language version). The contract should stipulate that after a set time (say, two years) all unused rights revert to you.
- **Your contract can also provide that publication rights revert to you if your novel goes out of print.** But how to define "out of print" in the age of Print on Demand? The Authors Guild suggests setting a minimum sales figure, and that your book should be in each edition of your publisher's catalog.
- **Your contract should state that all rights revert to you if the publisher files for bankruptcy, becomes insolvent or does not pay royalties in a timely manner.**

To Summarize, be prepared to negotiate for what you need:

- There should be specific contract language about the publisher's performance, such as how much editing and marketing support they commit to (including timing of edits), and your ability to provide input on title and cover (Ideally you will have veto power on both).
- If there is to be a print run, the publisher should commit to its size.
- The publisher should commit to distribute your book to physical and online stores.
- You should have the right to approve the final layout and edits on the book, and the publisher should consult with you regarding marketing.
- Any verbal representations the publisher makes during negotiations should be captured in the written contract.

Writer Commitments: There will also be specific contract language about your performance as a writer.

- You will commit to deliver the full manuscript by a set date. Given feedback from the publisher's editor, you will edit the manuscript within a set time (There may be several rounds for development, line edit and proofreading).
- If your manuscript includes any quotes from copyrighted sources, you will likely be expected to obtain (and pay for) permissions.
- You may be asked to assist in marketing your book by obtaining endorsements from reviewers and/or other authors for the back cover and other publicity materials.
- In general, you will likely be expected to collaborate with the publisher on publicity and marketing.
- The publisher may also ask for a right of first refusal on your future books. Be cautious about making such a commitment. Until you have actually worked through the cycle of publishing and marketing with this press, you do not know whether you would choose to publish with them again.

Advances and Royalties:

- **Negotiate Your Advance:** In setting the dollar figure for your advance, the number you and your publisher will aim to agree upon is the anticipated dollar figure for your first-year royalties. That is, *expected year one unit sales x price x royalty rate equals advance.* Let them propose a number and then you can explain why it should be higher. Your reasons may include some combination of your platform, your email list, your public appearances, your past publicity-related publications, and your endorsements. Publishers do not pay royalties until the accrued royalties exceed the advance, and so for many books the advance becomes the *de facto* total payment to the author. As a result, negotiating your advance is key. Negotiate for the advance to be paid half on signing, half on delivery of the final manuscript. Also negotiate for the advance to be non-refundable if the publisher fails to publish the book.

- **Negotiate Your Royalty Rate:** Typical royalty percentages vary by format (hardcover, paperback, audio). The percentages also vary depending on how they are calculated (list price of your book versus "net," where certain amounts are subtracted for things like anticipated returns from bookstores). If royalties in a contract are based on net sales, it is important to spell out exactly what can be subtracted. The Authors Guild keeps track of trends in those percentages. Their website is a great resource to learn more about this important subject (see the Resource List at the end of Part Three).

- **Payments:** The contract should state how often you will receive an accounting and any payment due. You should have the right to audit the publisher's accounting for your book.

- **Author's Copies:** The contract should stipulate that on publication you will receive a certain number of complimentary copies of your book (often 20-50). You can also negotiate for a lower per copy rate if you purchase additional copies later. Use these copies wisely. You may sell them, give them to reviewers and influencers, or provide at a discount to local bookclubs that invite you to speak.

Warranties and Indemnifications

- A publishing contract typically requires the author to represent that she did not plagiarize material in her book.

Typically the author agrees to take financial responsibility in a plagiarism lawsuit, but there should be limitations. Negotiate for language qualifying the representation you make by saying "to the best of the Author's knowledge." It's important to include that the publisher is responsible if a lawsuit is based on edits made by the publisher rather than material written by the author. In addition, the publisher probably carries liability insurance for plagiarism, and you can negotiate to be added to that policy. You can also negotiate for your liability in a plagiarism suit to be limited to the amount the publisher has paid you.
- It is especially important to seek legal advice regarding this technical area of Warranties and Indemnifications.

And remember: Anything the publisher promised you verbally should be captured in the written contract.

More resources about contracts are included in the Resource list at the end of Part Three.

After You Sign the Contract

Once both parties have signed the contract, the main steps involved in bringing your book to its final, publishable state are editing and production.

The Editing Phase

When you submitted your manuscript to your agent or publisher, it was already in the best shape you could possibly make it. You signed with a publisher to improve it even more.

The publisher's editor will evaluate your manuscript and will likely ask you to make additional edits based on their expertise. While you could ignore suggestions from your writing group with impunity, the edits proposed by your publisher are more than suggestions. This does not mean you must implement every change. If you have an objection to a change and a good reason, have an open-minded conversation with your editor. And if you retained an agent, they can advocate for you in conversations about changes.

Edits will likely be requested over several rounds:

- **Developmental Edits:** Your editor may suggest the addition of new material, or that you take a different approach to organizing your story. You are responsible to provide any new material that is needed.
- **Line Edits:** Your editor may suggest rewriting some sentences to eliminate awkward phrasing or cliched language. You are responsible for reviewing these edits and agreeing with them or discussing why they should not be incorporated.
- **Final Proofread:** This edit will re-check grammar, spelling, and punctuation, including in any newly written material. Be ready to discuss regional dialects or technical terms with which your proofreader may not be familiar. The final proofread will likely happen based on the Advance Review Copies, described below.

And, as described in Chapter Seventeen, during the editing phase of publication you will need to obtain permissions for any quotations that are not in the public domain.

The Production Phase

Once all edits are complete, the final manuscript will be formatted as a book for print and e-book versions. During production, the publisher will obtain ISBNs for each of your formats (see Chapter Seventeen for more about ISBNs).

Your publisher will engage a designer to create the cover for your book. Ideally you will have input into the instructions (called a "brief") given to your cover designer. You know your target market and the expectations of your genre, and if your contract is sound, you have approval rights (or at least consultation) on the cover of your book.

You will interact with the marketing team as they pull together material for the back cover. This will include a description based on your elevator pitch, as well as endorsements from reviewers or other authors, which you may be asked to obtain. Think ahead about who you would like to provide endorsements, especially if you have contacts who have written related books. It's great to use endorsements from authors with an established audience. Their endorsements can help them sell books too. Often, too, your editor will request blurbs from their stable of best-selling authors.

Production staff will create the look and feel for the interior of your book, and ideally you will be consulted. Your familiarity with expectations in the Seasoned Romance sub-genre will enable you to advise the publisher.

You will be asked for a professional quality headshot and a brief biography to include in your book and in publicity, such as a press release.

When the cover and interior are finalized except for the final proofread, the publisher will create Advance Review Copies (ARCs) which will be sent to reviewers and other media outlets as part of the publicity and marketing campaign for your book. These copies are clearly marked "ARC" and are not for sale. The final proofread will be based on the ARCs, and you will also be asked to read the final proof to spot any remaining errors before publication.

EXERCISE: CREATE YOUR AUTHOR BIOGRAPHY

Your author bio should connect you with the target audience for Well-Seasoned Romance, which will primarily be Romance readers of a certain age. Your bio should convey why these readers will enjoy your writing. Write in third person, beginning with a catchy first sentence. Be positive about yourself and your accomplishments. Make the tone of your bio consistent with the tone of your novel (If you wrote a gothic romance this time and plan a comedy next time, you'll rewrite your bio for the next book). End with a pitch: "She blogs at [website] and is on [social media platforms]. Follow her there."

Write a 100-word version, and then edit down to a 50-word version and a 25-word version. All three will come in handy for different purposes.

For an example, see my Author Bio at the end of this book.

THE POST-MORTEM: WOULD YOU WORK WITH THIS PUBLISHER AGAIN?

You will be busy with marketing and promotion for months after your launch date. When that activity calms down, take some time to reflect on your future. Assuming you did not commit to show your second novel to the same publisher, you will have many choices for your next novel. Those choices will include not only other traditional publishers, but also hybrid publishing and indie publishing, which may be more attractive given all that you have learned this time around. Consider these questions about your experience publishing this book:

- Did your publisher add value commensurate with taking 90% of the pie? Did they live up to their contract, or did you end up doing part of their job? Did they take the initiative and go the extra mile? Are you motivated to learn more about other publishers by discussing with other authors?
- Now that you understand more about a publisher's job, could you do parts of it? Do you want to? Read the chapter

on indie publishing and consider the pros and cons of that option.
- Or does the midrange possibility of hybrid publishing appeal to you? What tasks have you learned about during your experience with a traditional publisher that you could do yourself to bring down the costs of a hybrid press?

EXERCISE FOR TRADITIONAL PUBLISHING CHAPTER

Look in at least three traditionally published books that are comparable to yours. Note the agents and editors thanked in the Acknowledgements. Note the names of the publishers. Use this information to make a list of possible agents and/or publishers for further research.

<u>Bonus Exercise</u>: Sign up for a writing conference that includes opportunities to interact with agents and/or publishers. Be ready with the logline, tagline, and elevator pitch for your novel.

CHAPTER 19
HYBRID PUBLISHING

Back in the mid-twentieth century, long before Amazon, a writer who could not get a contract with a traditional publisher would sometimes use a "vanity press," meaning a printer for hire. Let's take a moment to unpack the term "vanity." There's the assumption that the writer's work was not good enough to publish, labeled with a word for a supposedly feminine failing. But was all the work from vanity presses really not good enough, or was some of it rejected due to bias in the publishing industry? In retrospect it's tough to say, because unlike the unvetted prose on Amazon, those early "vanity" works had a short shelf life.

It is ironic that long before the advent of modern publishing, everything was published by printers for hire. Shakespeare hired a printer; how often do you see his work labeled "vanity?"

But I digress. These days writers have several options beyond traditional publishing, and the option most likely to be confused with a vanity press is hybrid publishing. The two have a similar financial model: A hybrid press, like a vanity press, provides services for pay. But while a vanity press will print books for whoever can pay, regardless of content quality, a hybrid press is selective like a traditional publisher: It will only accept manuscripts that meet its editorial standards. And a hybrid press functions like a traditional press in providing editorial services, not just production services. Thus, hybrid publishing lies midway on a continuum from traditional to indie publishing.

There are still companies out there that function as vanity presses, publishing any book they are paid to produce. And to make things more confusing, these days such presses are likely to call themselves hybrid publishers. To assist writers in distinguishing the two, the Independent Book Publishers Association (IBPA) has compiled criteria for hybrids that writers can consider when choosing a publisher. These standards include vetting submissions for quality, providing a negotiable contract, publishing under their own imprint, and publishing to high editorial and production standards. Hybrid publishers also provide distribution services. And because they charge for services upfront, they pay royalties at significantly higher rates than traditional publishers. Reviewing the hybrid standards on the IBPA website (https://www.ibpa-online.org/page/hybrid-publisher-criteria-download) can help you develop questions to ask prospective publishers. Do your due diligence to determine whether a publisher's services meet your needs and whether their costs fit your budget.

- Ask for a sample contract and review it with your literary attorney.
- Review the publication steps in the indie publishing chapter so that you can ask in detail about editorial and production practices.
- Find out about distribution practices, including the hybrid publisher's track record at placing books in bookstores.
- Talk to other authors who have published recently with any hybrid you consider and find out whether there were hidden costs not disclosed in the contract.
- Ask whether these authors wish they had undertaken certain tasks themselves, rather than paying the press to perform them.

- And ask each hybrid press and the authors you speak with how long it takes this press from manuscript to launch. Is time to publication trending longer as the hybrid press becomes better known? While many hybrid presses publish more rapidly than their traditional counterparts, for some of the most popular hybrid publishers (such as SheWrites Press), publication can take just as long as going the traditional route.

The Hybrid Financial Model

Some hybrid presses provide a menu of services while others have a set package. Fees for a package of services can run anywhere from $3000 to $25,000 or higher, depending on the press.

On the other hand, the royalty percentage paid by a hybrid press is typically much higher than for a traditional press and can go as high as 80% (or more) of revenues received.

Disadvantages of a Hybrid Press

The cost of hybrid publishing is a clear disadvantage compared with traditional or indie publication. Especially when working with a higher end publisher, authors who publish with a hybrid press may not break even on their investment. In addition, some hybrid publishers do not provide marketing support, and authors must pay separately for those services.

Another disadvantage is difficulty accessing reviewers and literary prizes. Books that are traditionally published benefit from an assumption of legitimacy which indie books often lack. Books published under the hybrid model fall somewhere in the middle. Some but not all reviewers and awards that are closed to indie published books do consider books from hybrid publishers.

Advantages of a Hybrid Press

Time to publication can be a big advantage. With some hybrid publishers, publication can occur in months, as opposed to two years or more with a traditional publisher. I've spoken with women writers over sixty who are unwilling to wait years to see their books in print. As this publication model becomes more popular, however, the difference in timing can shrink. Be sure to inquire of each hybrid press you speak with about recent times to publication.

Another advantage of the hybrid model is that authors can exercise more control over the final product than they could with a traditional publisher. Decisions like cover design are typically more collaborative than with a traditional press.

Plus, the faster timeline and greater control is achieved without you having to learn all the skills involved in indie publishing. The hybrid publisher takes on everything from buying ISBNs to formatting the book to distribution. Authors who make this choice often say the cost is worth it.

There is also a level of camaraderie among the authors I know at SheWrites that I've not seen among authors at traditional presses. These women go on retreats together, promote one another's books on social media, and support one another's success. This may or may not be true for other hybrid presses.

The Hybrid Publishing Contract

> Reminder: I am not an attorney and the information below is not legal advice. I am only sharing what I wish I had known at the outset of my writing career. Please consult a literary attorney before signing a publishing contract.

Please review the contract portion of the Traditional Publishing chapter to familiarize yourself with the standard provisions of a publishing contract including the Grant of Rights, the obligations of the publisher and the obligations of the writer. The contract with a hybrid publisher will reflect the differences in approach from the traditional publishing model.

Because one advantage of a hybrid press is greater collaboration with the author on choices such as cover design, the contract should reflect the areas where the author will have consultation or even veto rights regarding the final manuscript. And as noted above, the hybrid model has a different financial arrangement that will be captured in the contract: The author commits to invest in the publishing process, there is no advance to the author, and the royalty percentage paid to the author is much higher than with a traditional publisher.

Different hybrid publishers take different approaches to providing services. Some offer a standard package similar to the services provided by a traditional publisher. Other hybrid presses offer a menu of services with the contract priced according to the author's choices. And to be sure that there won't be any unwelcome surprises during and after publication, make sure that the contract covers all steps in the process — or be prepared to pay separately for ARCs, ISBNs, shipping, marketing, etc.

If you choose a hybrid publisher with an a la carte menu of services, consider which functions you could perform yourself to lower your costs. And as with any contract, verbal commitments should be captured in writing.

EXERCISE: COMPARING PUBLISHING MODELS

Hybrid publishing is similar to traditional publishing in many ways, and similar to indie publishing in others. Be sure to review both the traditional and indie publishing chapters to understand your full range of choices.

- Make a list of what you like best, and least, about each of the three publishing pathways.
- Now choose the key pluses and minuses for each. Which pathway seems most appealing? (You can, of course, pitch your book to both traditional and hybrid publishers.)

CHAPTER 20
INDIE PUBLISHING

The decision to self-publish puts you in charge. In effect, you are running your own business, not just being an author. You control the quality of the product, the timing to publication, and every creative and business decision along the way. And in addition, you are accountable for publicity and marketing. This route to publication gives you maximum freedom and maximum responsibility—which could be good news or bad news, depending on your preferences.

Here are the steps involved in indie publishing, some of which can happen in parallel.

Finalize Your Manuscript

By now you have probably read your manuscript a dozen times, including reading it out loud (or engaging AI to read it to you). You have had friends and Beta readers give you feedback, and if you are in a writing group, they have read and opined on part or all of your book. Some of your friends may be experienced proofreaders who deserve a big thank-you and two dozen cookies (as do all your pre-readers, actually).

All that is great. But before your manuscript leaves the nest, consider hiring a professional editor to check for problems others may have missed, either at the developmental, line edit, or proofreading stages. If you choose to hire an editor, do your due diligence first. Ask for a sample edit of a few pages of your work. Talk with their references (other authors whose work they have edited) and check those books for quality of editing. Be sure you understand the full scope of costs you will need to pay.

And of course, read your book yourself one last time. I was amazed by the little things I caught at the last minute in *Vampires of a Certain Age*.

Front and Back Matter

A professional-looking book also includes **Front and Back Matter**, which is the information that appears before and after the story itself. For *Vampires of a Certain Age*, for example, the front matter includes:

- Title Page.
- Copyright Page.
- Table of Contents.
- Quote (from a poem by Queen Elizabeth I).

If your book has a Dedication, that could also appear in in the Front Matter.

The Back Matter for *Vampires* includes:

- A page inviting readers to follow my blogs at www.stellafosse.com.
- Acknowledgements.
- About the Author (Brief biography with a headshot).
- Also by Stella Fosse (List of previous books).
- Author's Note (An explanation of why I wanted to write this book, and my relevant background in blood banking etc.).
- A page inviting readers to write online reviews.

- A Discussion Guide for book clubs.

The bio and headshot could have appeared on the back cover instead—your choice. Take a look at the Front and Back Matter for books you have on hand, including Seasoned Romance novels. From there, decide what you would like to include in your novel, and in what order.

Buy ISBN Numbers

To enable buyers to find and order your novel, you will need a unique International Standard Book Number for each format of your book (hardcover, paperback, eBook, audio book, etc.). To buy ISBNs, you'll need a publishing company name, so choose a name for your imprint that you will be comfortable using for future books.

The authorized seller of ISBNs in the United States is a company called Bowker. ISBNs from other sellers continue to belong to those sellers. Bowker sells ISBNs singly or in blocks of 10 and 100, depending on how optimistic you are about your writing career.

If you decide to publish *only* on Amazon, it has its own numbering system for books called ASINs. (See discussion below regarding the pros and cons of Amazon exclusive publication).

Using non-Bowker numbers can be limiting. Be aware that many independent booksellers won't stock books with an Amazon ASIN.

For more about ISBNs, please refer back to Chapter Sixteen.

Obtain a Great Cover Design

Despite the old saying, people do judge a book by its cover, and yours will be no different. You want a cover that tracks expectations for the Seasoned Romance sub-genre, that is compelling even in a thumbnail view, and that works for your particular book.

- **Genre Expectations:** Just as readers expect a certain structure to the Romance narrative, they expect certain elements on the cover of a Romance. And those expectations have changed in recent years. The photographic "clinch" covers of the late twentieth century have largely been replaced by pop abstracts with bright colors: pinks, yellows, light purples and teals. Most Romance covers from the 2020s do feature characters, but they tend to emphasize the joy in relationship as opposed to overtly sexual images. However, the covers of paranormal Romances (like *Vampires of a Certain Age*) still use darker colors, and often use photos versus drawings of characters. The transition away from pecs and abs works well for Seasoned Romance, given our society's obsession with the younger body. A cover that featured a bare-chested 70-year-old man might trigger unconscious bias in the staunchest anti-ageism activist. So what do we see on Seasoned Romance covers these days? Recent covers by authors like Maggie Christensen, Meka James and Lina Rehal feature hands clinking wineglasses, flowers against colorful backgrounds, and stylized figures of older characters. It's worth your time to acquaint yourself with evolving expectations. One place to begin: Join the Seasoned Romance group on Facebook and look at their weekly feature on new releases. Or look online at covers of books by some of the authors in the Resource list at the end of Part One. Or just search "Later in Life Romance" on Amazon and check out the covers of the current top sellers.

- **Thumbnail View:** As you plan your design, think about visibility. A thumbnail version of your cover is the first thing your potential readers will see. Bold strokes will show up much better in thumbnail than small details, long titles, or lengthy subtitles.
- **The Right Cover for Your Particular Book:** Consider the themes in your book, its location in time and space, and the mood you want to convey. This will be particular to your novel. *Vampires of a Certain Age*, for example, is a gothic

Seasoned Romance, so it is thematically darker than most Seasoned Romance novels. I wanted to show Marion (Character A in the novel) on the night in the 1500s when she transitioned from mortal to vampire. The character is in her late thirties, but that was the end of the typical lifespan in that era. Diana Rosinus Studios created a cover that gives Marion a young-and-old appearance. And in line with the expectations for the paranormal romance genre, the design places her firmly in a medieval setting. That novel is the first in the planned "Matriarchal Vampire" series, and covers for upcoming books will echo the medieval archway that frames Marion. In the future, if I write contemporary Seasoned Romance novels, I will opt for brighter and more stylized covers in keeping with current Seasoned Romance expectations.

- **Back Cover**: You will need a back cover for your print version but not for your e-book. Check published books to see the typical layout. The text on the back of your print version will include a description of your book (You can use or modify the Elevator Pitch you developed in Chapter Ten). You will also need endorsements from reviewers or other authors, which you should request when you send out your Advance Review Copies. The ISBN appears on the back cover along with the price of the book. You may also choose to include your professional quality author headshot. And to finalize the cover, you will set up the spine with your name and the title of the book. The width of the spine will depend on the page count of your book.
- **Find the Right Cover Designer**: Look in the Acknowledgements sections of books with covers you like to find names of cover designers. Or if you have an artistic bent, consider using a tool like Canva to create your Seasoned Romance cover. If you are on a budget, look at online sites that advertise less expensive covers—but shop carefully to ensure you get a cover that meets your

requirements, meets genre expectations and will attract your target audience. Watch out for sites that sell the same few covers with slight variations.

AUTHOR'S CRAFT: CREATE A BRIEF FOR YOUR COVER DESIGNER

When it is time to hire a cover designer, put together a brief that suits the genre and your particular book. Here is what your designer needs to know:

- The title of your book, and your name (or pen name).
- The logline, tagline and elevator pitch for your book (use the work you did in Chapter Ten).
- Examples of Seasoned Romance covers: Download online cover images for comparable books that appeal to you based on colors, font, and themes, as well as their depiction of characters, objects and backgrounds.
- Your Target Audience: Given that you are writing about characters after midlife, this is especially important if your cover designer is much younger. Let your designer know that your readers (and your characters) are vivid and engaged. Think Joan Price (editor of *Ageless Erotica*), not the stereotyped frail senior citizen.
- Comparable Authors: Share who else in the Seasoned Romance sub-genre is writing stories that are somewhat similar to yours in setting and theme.
- To finalize your full wraparound cover, your designer will also need all the materials that belong on the spine and back cover materials (text, ISBN, price, and headshot if you are including it). You'll also need to state the number of pages so that the designer can create the right spine width.

- Be clear that you own the resulting images. In some states a "work for hire" arrangement must be spelled out in a contract with specific language. Speak with your literary attorney about this.
- Tell your designer all the formats and sizes required. For example, if you are producing both printed copies and e-books, your designer will need to provide versions with two different color spaces (These are known as Cyan, Magenta, Yellow and Black (CMYK) for print and Red, Green, Blue (RGB) for online and ebook).

> If you are hiring contract workers such as a cover designer, be sure your agreements cover your needs for quality, revisions, timing, and ensure your ownership of all resulting Intellectual Property.

Produce and Distribute Your Novel

When it is time to format your manuscript and produce the publishable version, you have decisions to make, based in part on your budget. If you decide to publish only on Amazon, their website has tools that will enable you to convert your Word document into a publishable manuscript for little or no money. Kindle Create, the Amazon formatting application, is relatively simple to use and provides chapter templates. You can also use an Amazon number (ASIN) for your book instead of buying an ISBN, but you won't be able to sell your book elsewhere.

You may want to publish beyond Amazon, to online stores such as Barnes & Noble, AppleBooks, and Kobo. This wider publication will help you reach a larger audience and establish a following. To publish beyond Amazon you will need a formatting program, such as Vellum (for Mac computers) or Atticus (windows or Mac). Be sure to do your editing in Word before you transfer your manuscript to the formatting program, as these programs are not as edit-friendly.

Once your manuscript including front and back matter is fully formatted with your final cover, you can generate Advance Review Copies (ARCs) for reviewers and other marketing uses discussed in Part Four. Add a banner to the front cover saying "Advance Review Copy - Not For Sale." If you are sending ARCs to the people writing back cover blurbs for your novel, it is fine to leave room for those endorsements on the ARC version of the back cover. You can also note on the back cover that the final proofread is still to be performed; the ARC may be the version you send to a professional proofreader.

After the final proofread it is time to create your finished book. Add the back cover endorsements and ISBN, remove the ARC sticker, and you are ready to launch. You can distribute the e-book format of your novel across multiple platforms yourself, or work with a service called an *aggregator* to publish wide. There are several aggregators to choose from and they typically charge 10-15% of author revenues for this service. You can distribute the print version of your book via a Print on Demand source such as Ingram Spark.

Distributing your print book to physical bookstores as an indie author is challenging. If that is one of your goals, find bookstores in your area that champion local authors. Start buying your books from those stores. Get to know the staff, including the book buyer and the person who organizes events. Bring them print ARCs of your book. Chat with them about hosting an event there. Ask if they would consider stocking your book, possibly on a consignment basis (Read more about launch events in Part Four).

PART THREE: CONCLUSION & RESOURCES

Choosing a publishing route takes time and reflection. Before you commit to a publishing pathway for your first Well-Seasoned Romance, talk with traditional publishers, hybrid publishers, and also service providers such as freelance editors and cover designers. You may change your mind depending on what you learn.

Once you have settled on a pathway and are choosing a particular publisher (or choosing service providers, if you go indie), be sure you speak with authors who have used their services recently. Publishers and service providers change over time in ways that can affect your experience.

And lastly, because the publishing industry is in flux, it is important to keep up with trends. Follow sites like the Authors Guild and Jane Friedman's blog to learn what's happening now. See the Resource List, below.

And as discussed in Part One, it is never too soon to begin planning the publicity and marketing for your novel. Your transition from writer to author begins the day you write the first sentence of your book. Much more to come on that topic just ahead in Part Four.

PART THREE RESOURCES

General Publishing Resources

Jane Friedman (https://janefriedman.com/) writes about the book publishing industry and helps authors understand changes in the business. Her resources include:

- Jane's blog (https://janefriedman.com/blog/) about the industry which is free to subscribe.
- *The Business of Being a Writer* (https://janefriedman.com/books/) is Jane's book, which as of this writing is being updated for a new 2025 edition.
- Jane's guide (https://janefriedman.com/sample-permission-letter/) to Fair Use and sample permission letter. Useful if you would like to quote material from another author that is not in the public domain.

Facebook groups to check current trends in themes and cover design for Seasoned Romance include:

- Seasoned Romance (https://www.facebook.com/groups/958318970951705).
- Authors of Seasoned Romance (https://www.facebook.com/groups/2480800365515225).
- Seasoned Romance Salon (https://www.facebook.com/groups/1186759005074875).

Writers Beware has useful information about publishing scams. (www.writersbeware.blog).

And this is a fun presentation about Romance covers (https://pudding.cool/2023/10/romance-covers/).

Traditional and Hybrid Publishing Resources

The Authors Guild (https://authorsguild.org/) is a great resource as you choose and work with a publishing option.

- Non-members can access their model book contract and background information about book contracts.
- Members can also obtain a contract review from a Guild literary attorney.

Resources to find potential agents and publishers:

- Manuscript Wishlist: A searchable site where agents and publishers looking for submissions post their manuscript wishes (www.mswishlist.com).
- Duotrope: Resource to search for agents and publishers. Charges but has a free trial period. (www.duotrope.com)
- Agent Query: (www.AgentQuery.com).
- Query Tracker: (www.QueryTracker.net).
- Writer's Market: (https://writersmarket.com).
- Literary Marketplace: (https://www.literarymarketplace.com/lmp/us/index_us.asp).

Independent Book Publishers Association Standards for hybrid Publishers: (www.ibpa-online.org/page/hybrid-publisher-criteria-download).

Indie Publishing Resources

International Standard Book Numbers:

The Bowker website (www.bowker.com/isbn-us) for purchasing ISBNs in the United States

Here is information from some of the online stores on how to upload your novel:

- Amazon: (https://kdp.amazon.com/en_US/help/topic/G200641240).
- Barnes and Noble: (https://press.barnesandnoble.com/how-it-works).
- Apple Books: (https://authors.apple.com/epub-upload).
- Kobo: (https://pressbooks.howardcc.edu/guide/chapter/getting-your-book-into-ebook-stores-kobo/).
- Google Play: (https://play.google.com/store/books).
- Draft2Digital is an example of an aggregator that will publish e-books to multiple platforms: (https://draft2digital.com)

IngramSpark is an example of a resource for print on demand and distribution to online and physical bookstores: (www.ingramspark.com).

PART FOUR: SELL YOUR WELL-SEASONED ROMANCE

CHAPTER 21
OVERVIEW OF PUBLICITY AND MARKETING

Of all the jobs an author has, the one that might come least naturally is selling books. Marketing is *not* why most of us became writers. Selling may feel unseemly, like descending from an ivory tower to hawk used cars. But no matter which publishing route you choose, marketing must be part of the plan if you are to succeed.

You might have the impression that your traditional publisher will take sole responsibility for marketing your book. That might have been true in the era when big publishing houses chauffeured their best-selling authors from one reading to the next. The reality today is different. Most debut authors — even those lucky enough to sign with a major New York publisher — discover that they themselves are an integral part of the marketing team for their novel. And those of us who publish independently are in charge of all marketing as well as writing.

Bottom line: Ultimately it is your job to sell your books. Yes, marketing takes time away from writing, and it's important to find a balance. But no matter how you launch your books into the world, at some point you'll transition from writer to author: from someone who writes to someone who writes and sells. The earlier you start the better, and you can find ways to make it fun: to share your voice with your readers and engage with them in authentic ways.

The Transition from Writer to Author

To be an author requires a shift in perspective so that you see your book as a product. That requires both a change in mindset and the development of new skills. In Part One you began to create your author brand.

- You built a website and began blogging.
- You started a mailing list to reach your followers directly.
- You connected with potential readers on social media and in real life.
- You wrote basic marketing tools for your novel (logline, tagline, elevator pitch) that focused your writing and supplied the foundation for marketing and publicity.

And if you pitched your book to traditional or hybrid publishers, you developed more marketing tools in Part Three: a query letter and a synopsis.

In the chapters ahead you will continue that shift into authorship. You will assess your strengths and decide which types of publicity and marketing are right for you and your book. You will build on your brand, expand your author platform, continue on the path of good literary citizenship, and develop your marketing plan.

Publicity versus Marketing

The terms "publicity" and "marketing" are often conflated, but they mean different things. Publicity covers a wide range of unpaid promotion for your novel. Marketing includes both strategic planning for the success of your book and paid advertising.

Publicity: There are many ways to get the word out without spending a dime, starting with writing and sharing a press release.

Other types of publicity include writing guest articles, sharing professional and reader book reviews, holding launch events, appearing on podcasts, and giving readings at local venues such as bookstores and libraries. Publicity includes getting the word out using your social media platform, your blog, and your mailing list. Your success with free publicity will depend on your network of contacts. In Chapter 21 you will learn about creative ways to leverage your platform to reach readers.

Marketing includes both advertising and strategizing, such as optimizing keywords and tracking the effectiveness of different promotions. Tracking is especially important if the money paying for marketing is your own. Marketing also includes strategic decisions like the price of your book and how you distribute it—all part of planning for the success of your novel. Advertising means *paid* promotion for your book. How much of this you do will depend on your budget. Possibilities include print and digital advertising, book giveaways, a book trailer and book swag (such as custom bookmarks, stickers and postcards). In Chapter 22 you will learn more about marketing options and create your plan.

Creating a Marketing Plan

Review the materials in the next two chapters and consider which possibilities best fit your skills, your budget, your audience and your book. That will prepare you to build a marketing plan for your Seasoned Romance. The plan is a living document that will change over the course of your marketing campaign as you learn what's working and what is not—and as you learn new skills and expand your abilities. There are many possible ways to market your novel, and no one can do them all. But knowing your skills, your book, and your preferences will enable you to set priorities.

Before you plunge into the nitty-gritty of publicity in Chapter 21, take a look at the exercise below. These questions will prompt you to start exploring possibilities.

EXERCISE: PUBLICITY AND MARKETING QUESTIONS FOR YOUR NOVEL

Take notes on the ideas below that appeal to you. This is the start of building your marketing plan.

- Why did you write this Well-Seasoned Romance?
- What nonfiction articles could you write that relate to your book, and where would you submit them for publication?
- Make a list of questions about your book that might engage book club readers.
- Where could you send press releases about your novel? (Don't underestimate the power of local media.)
- List five reasons why booksellers might want to stock your book.
- What are your three best comps (books similar to yours that have sold well)?
- What creative venues might host a reading for your book? (For example, if one of your protagonists is a baker, consider bakeries.)
- Where could you go on book tour? (Think about venues in towns you're planning to visit in the year after launch.)
- What book festivals are happening in your region in the coming year?
- Which of your friends might be willing to host a reading in their homes and invite their other friends?
- Have you ever made an Instagram reel? Would you like to learn?
- Do you enjoy creating graphics? Ever played with designs on Canva?
- What advertising budget would be comfortable for you?

In the next chapter, we will delve into more publicity ideas for your Well-Seasoned Romance. Onward!

CHAPTER 22
PUBLICIZE YOUR BOOK

You can do a lot to publicize your book that does not involve spending money. Some things are essential, like the creation of book ordering pages for the online stores where you sell your book. The choice of other publicity avenues will depend on your preferences, skills, and available time, as well as the content and themes of your book. As you read the options below, consider which ones appeal to you, and which ones would be stretch goals. The more publicity you create, the better; yet there is always a need to balance your time between publicity for this book and writing your next book.

If you are with a traditional publisher, in the best case the publicity staff will arrange for you to write guest articles and be interviewed on podcasts and videocasts. They may also arrange for reviews in publications and for launch events at local bookstores. But even if your traditional publisher is adept at publicity, you will be expected to use your contacts to arrange for more. Here are some ways you can publicize your book.

Keep Building Audience and Network

Blogs: As you move toward publication, think about blog topics that fit well with your upcoming book. Consider inviting guest bloggers (especially other authors) whose themes mesh with yours. You may wish to swap guest posts with them. Follow and boost podcasts on related themes, and mention your new book as you go.

Mailing List: Your mailing list is a key asset: a guaranteed way to reach a pool of potential buyers for your books. Keep giving people reasons to sign up and make it easy to do so. Create a pop-up window on your blogs that offers folks a chance to submit their email address, so they will keep seeing your blogs and newsletters. Develop a "Thank you" for new subscribers (such as a free short story). Share the link to each new blog across social media. And keep the people on your mailing list up to date about your events and publications.

Outreach: Also consider new ways to connect with other writers. Is there an umbrella writers' organization in your state? A local chapter of Romance Writers of America? What Facebook groups for Seasoned Romance can you follow? What other organizations could be useful (Romance Writers of America; Women Fiction Writers Association; Association of Writers and Writing Programs, etc.)? With whom could you trade reviews, blurbs, social media mentions? How well do you know the owner of your local bookstore? Do you enjoy going to readings?

EXERCISE: CONTINUING TO NETWORK

Your Audience: Review who you see as your potential readers, and answer these questions.

- Who is most likely to be interested in what you are writing? Think demographics, and also interest in the settings and themes in your book.
- Where do those folks congregate, both online and in person?

- What social media platforms do your potential readers frequent?
- How can you address the needs of readers in the niche of Well-Seasoned Romance?

Your Influencers: Write down five or more people who are influential regarding the subjects and themes you write about (check the Resource List at the end of Part One for examples of authors). Find these people online. Are they on LinkedIn? Facebook? Instagram? If you're not already connected with them, please connect now. Comment on their posts and re-share them with your own commentary. If you see an article in the media that might interest an influencer, send them a message.

Cover Reveal

Your cover is the face of your book. Announce that your cover is coming on your social media platform. Then share it, and share your excitement about it, on your cover reveal day. Be sure to thank your fabulous designer.

Create and Distribute a Press Release and Press Kit

A press release is a sort of birth announcement before the fact. Once your Advance Review Copies are out, and when you have the first praise from other authors, set up a Word document with the essential elements of your press release.

- Book launch date.
- Front cover.
- Publication Formats (e.g., paperback, e-book, audio).
- ISBN for each format.
- Distribution (online stores? Ingram Spark? Draft2Digital? Others?).

- Price.
- Word and/or Page Count.
- Genre / Sub-genre (Seasoned Romance; Late in Life Romance).
- Logline, Tagline, Elevator Pitch.
- Author Headshot (Best if professional, but you can use a good cell phone photo if necessary).
- Advance Praise (see section below on asking for reviews).
- About the Author, including web and social information (see Author's Craft section on writing your brief biography, Chapter Eighteen).
- Contact Information.

Here is the press release for *Vampires of a Certain Age* that you can use as a template for your release. It is included in the download pack that you can get at https://stellafosse.com/wsrdownload.

PRESS RELEASE

Chapel Hill, North Carolina, August 2023

Baubo Books Announces Publication of:

Vampires of a Certain Age
Five Hundred Years of Loving

by Stella Fosse

Paperback [Distributed by Ingram Spark] ISBN: 978-1-950227-09-9, $15.95
E-Book [on all major platforms] ISBN: 978-1-950227-08-2, $5.99
52000 Words / 230 Pages
Publication Date: September 15, 2023

ABOUT THE BOOK:

A medieval healer turned vampire finds her true calling in a 21st century blood bank, where she falls in love with the one person who could destroy her.

Marion Chase is an herbal healer in medieval Yorkshire. Falsely accused of witchcraft after falling for her closest friend, she is ostracized by the Church and persecuted by her fellow villagers. Rescued by a vampire and now immortal, Marion joins a sanctuary in York dedicated to virtuous living for vampires. Centuries and many adventures later, Marion finds her true calling as president of a Chicago blood bank, providing ethically sourced blood to Midwestern vampires. There she falls in love with a powerful adversary: Rachel Sutter, an FDA agent and the living likeness of Marion's medieval love.

Women who enjoy vampire stories will be delighted with this nerdy lesbian romance. Join author Stella Fosse to explore the romantic life of a powerful 500-year-old female vampire.

ADVANCE PRAISE FOR *VAMPIRES OF A CERTAIN AGE*:

A book filled with romance and dark secrets that will keep you turning the pages!
--Danielle Paquette-Harvey, Author of *The Goddess' Wards*

Delightfully fresh. Stella Fosse's style is crisp visually as well as verbally. Ethically sourced blood is the best thing since "What We Do in the Shadows!"
--Diana Wilde, Host of "Granny's Got a Podcast!"

Stella Fosse is an incredible writer. There is subtle beauty in the romantic elements.
-- J.H. Laing, author of *Bound* and *Unraveled* of the *Tethered Souls* Series

Cont…..

Review copies are available upon request in ePub, PDF or print.

PRESS RELEASE

Vampires of a Certain Age moves seamlessly between sixteenth century England and the present-day USA. In its well-paced and dramatic events, we see the strength of the personal bonds between women and the persecution from authorities over time. Running throughout is the blood of life.
--Stephanie Shields, Author of *The Strange Woman*

A brilliant twist on the vampire myth, told from a feminist perspective.
--Mirinda Kossoff, Author of *The Rope of Life*

Stella Fosse's book brings to life a coven of vampires searching for a way to live and do no harm. *Vampires of a Certain Age* brings us the matriarchal vampire.
--Margo Arrowsmith, Host of the "Age Out Loud" Podcast

ABOUT THE AUTHOR:

Stella Fosse is the *nom de plume* of a sixty-something author who writes sexy stories as a creative antidote to the gendered ageism women face in society. She champions older women's creativity by leading workshops in seasoned romance, erotica, and memoir writing. Stella is a frequent guest on podcasts for women past midlife and is published in many online venues. She blogs about issues of interest to Women of a Certain Age, including creativity, romance, and older women's health.

Traditionally published works include Stella's book *Aphrodite's Pen: The Power of Writing Erotica after Midlife*. Her story collection, *The Erotic Pandemic Ball*, is an imaginative exploration of romance in quarantine. Her first novel, *Brilliant Charming Bastard*, is a romantic escapade through the San Francisco biotech scene. Her second novel, *Vampires of a Certain Age*, celebrates the love life of a powerful 500-year-old woman.

Stella's books are available at your local independent or chain bookseller and your favorite online place.
She shares her writing, as well as ideas and resources to empower women past midlife, at www.stellafosse.com.
You can also find Stella Fosse on:
- Facebook: facebook.com/StellaFosseAuthor
- Instagram: instagram.com/stella.fosse
- Twitter: twitter.com/stellafosse
- LinkedIn: linkedin.com/in/StellaFosse

Please join her there.

CONTACT:
Contact publicist Graham Bird at +1 (415) 999-3106 and graham@stellafosse.com

Mailing Address: Baubo Books, 125 S. Estes Drive #4311, Chapel Hill, North Carolina 27514, USA.

End.

Review copies are available upon request in ePub, PDF or print.

Send your press release to media outlets such as podcasters and your local newspaper. Even better, send a full press kit, which could include:

- Your press release.
- The offer of a Review Copy (ebook or print).

- A page with the title of your book and its table of contents.
- A brief excerpt from your novel.
- A page of suggested interview questions (see sample later in this chapter).

Set Up Online Book Pages (and Author Pages)

Your book pages on internet stores such as Barnes & Noble and Amazon showcase your new Well-Seasoned Romance. You can set up your sales pages on online stores to accept pre-orders. On Amazon, for example, book sales on the first day drive how likely the site is to show your book to prospective readers. Reminding your online following to pre-order your book can boost your sales.

Each online store has its own requirements for book pages (see the Resource list at the end of Part Four for links). Your logline, tagline, pitch, author biography, and headshot are all essential components. You should also post early reviews (see below).

Ask for Book Reviews

As you build your social media network and participate in writing conferences, you will meet other authors who may be willing to write endorsements for your book. This is a wonderful thing we can do for each other. Use these endorsements on the back cover of your book, in memes you post on social media, and in your press kit. Consider your press release a living document and update it as endorsements come in. Keep building relationships with other authors and find ways to support one another.

> Pro Tip: Romance readers read lots of Romance novels. Your partnerships with other Romance authors are a win/win for everyone.

Online reviews from readers are also important to sales. Don't be shy about asking your Beta readers to review your book on Amazon, Barnes & Noble, BookBub, Goodreads, and wherever else they review books. Once you launch and readers are buying your book, remind them periodically on your platform and in your newsletter that reviews are essential to make your book visible through online stores. How likely the sales algorithms are to display your book to new readers depends partly on the number of reviews. These need not be lengthy; a single sentence plus a rating will do. A sustained pattern of reviews can be more effective than a single burst of reviews at launch.

Leverage Your Blog and Mailing List

In addition to publishing your blog on a regular schedule, consider publishing a monthly newsletter where you share what's happening with your writing and publishing projects. Start talking about your book in your newsletter while you are still writing and editing. Let your readers know why you are writing this book, who your main characters are, and what the conflict is that powers your story. Write blogs that connect with the settings and themes of your book and mention your book in the process. Some writers share excerpts of their books in progress; some even ask their readership to vote on plot direction.

Pitch Your Book on Social Media

Consider which social media platforms make sense to pitch your book. Instagram is highly visual; LinkedIn has many users past midlife; Facebook has many niche audience groups. Join the ones you will keep up with on a regular basis.

Believe it or not, publicity can be creative. Here are some fun ways to pitch your book on social media.

- **Memes:** You can set up a basic account on Canva.com for free and use it to create colorful graphics with brief quotes

from your book, as well as quotes from early reviews. These graphics are great to share on Instagram and can also be eye-catching on other social media sites. Be sure to include ordering information (or another "ask," such as "Join my mailing list") in the caption.
- **Reels:** Using your cell phone, record a brief plug for your book. This can be just ten seconds about why your readers will enjoy your story. Or read a captivating sentence or two.
- **Photos:** Did you travel to the location where your book is set? I had fun posting pictures of the walled city of York, where much of *Vampires of a Certain Age* takes place. My favorite was a recumbent medieval tombstone with a hole drilled in the stone to accommodate a stake. Your comments on your photos are a great place to publicize your book (Book trailers, which require buying video software, are covered in the Marketing chapter).

When it comes to social media posts, be a good literary citizen. Give more than you ask, and "pay it forward" well before you need to ask for something from your followers. You may be tempted to jump on your platform every day and beg people to buy your book. Don't do it. Even though you've made the cutest memes and the best reels, you will turn people off if that's all you share. Try posting about your book every fifth day, alternating various memes, reels, and photos. On the other days, continue to praise other authors and to post articles of interest to your audience.

Pitch Guest Articles on Related Topics

One publicity avenue that comes naturally to writers is writing guest articles for publications, including others' blogs. Consider publications that relate to the setting or time period for your book. For example, I worked in biotechnology for decades and *Vampires of a*

Certain Age is partly set in a blood bank. If I were to write an article for a blood bank trade magazine, I would mention my novel in the author bio for the article.

Also consider pitching an article about writing a Well-Seasoned Romance, or an article about why our love lives are vital and important after sixty. There are a number of blogs and online magazines about women after midlife and many of these welcome guest essays (see the Resource list at the end of Part Four). On my website, for example, I typically publish a guest blog by a woman author over fifty on the tenth of each month. These guest essays can cover topics such as why the author wrote her book and what it means to share a creative voice later in life. I look forward to hearing from you when your novel launches!

There are other creative ways to promote your novel through writing adjacent to your book. For example, you could write a short story that is a spinoff from your book. Submit it to contests or provide it free to your mailing list as an enticement to buy your novel. You can also write brief backgrounds about your characters and make them available via social media in exchange for email addresses to add to your mailing list.

Ask Podcasters for Guest Spots

There is a terrific bumper crop of podcasts by and for Women of a Certain Age. Build your network with the hosts of these shows. Check out episodes of podcasts from the Resource List at the end of Part Four and promote episodes you like on your social media platform. Connect with hosts and thank them for what they're doing.

These podcasts are great places to ask for a guest spot to talk about your Seasoned Romance. You may not be accustomed to public appearances, but these are friendly venues and they will make you feel right at home. As you watch and listen to episodes, get a sense of whether there might be a fit with your book. Then reach out via email with a cordial note and attach your press kit. Ask if they would like a complimentary e-copy of your book, and let them know you would love an invitation to their show.

The more you appear on podcasts the more comfortable you will become with the experience of being interviewed. The first few times, ask your host ahead of time for questions they are likely to ask you. Write down your answers and practice them before your appearance. You will find over time that similar questions pop up from different interviewers, and you'll become more comfortable ad libbing responses. You can also create a list of suggested questions, include it in your press kit, and share it with interviewers ahead of time. Below is the interview list I generated for *Vampires of a Certain Age*.

Sample Interview Questions

(Provided to Interviewers for *Vampires of a Certain Age*)

1. You typically write about powerful older women. Why write a vampire novel?

2. Why did you call your book *Vampires of a Certain Age*?

3. What do you see as the main themes in your novel?

4. What exactly is "ethically sourced blood?"

5. Your main character, Marion Chase, is five hundred years old. How is that different from being an older mortal woman?

6. Your other main character, Rachel Sutter, is in her fifties and is the younger woman in the central romance. Why was that important?

7. Your first novel, *Brilliant Charming Bastard*, took place in a biotech startup. This novel is set partly in a blood bank. Why the focus on science in your books?

8. What are you hearing from early readers of *Vampires of a Certain Age*?

9. What's next? Are you planning a movie script? Who would you cast as Marion and Rachel?

10. Will there be a sequel? Is this the start of a series?

Podcasts are usually recorded and edited to post later. When one of your interviews launches, share the link across your platform and thank your host in your caption. Add an Events tab to your author website and post links to all your appearances so that your readers can check out recordings later.

The Resource List at the end of Part Four includes podcasts you might consider. The first part of the list is podcasts that focus on Women of a Certain Age; the second part is podcasts about the Romance genre. The list is current as of this writing, but over time new podcasts will appear and others may stop producing, so do look online for new opportunities. Before you write to a podcast host, be sure to check out several episodes so that you can tell the host why you're excited to appear on their particular show.

Podcasts are also great practice for larger appearances, such as speaking at conferences and on radio and television. Start small and work your way up the ladder of free publicity.

> Pro Tip: If you are not comfortable with public appearances, consider joining a local chapter of Toastmasters for a free, low-stress way to practice your oratory skills.

Plan Your Launch (and Other Events)

A launch party is great fun and a terrific opportunity to take pictures for your website. A bookstore launch is customary and can be a blast. If you are traditionally published, your publisher may have a good relationship with a bookstore near you. Even a traditional publisher may tell you, however, that such events generate fewer sales than you expect. If you are doing your own publicity, it's a good idea to cultivate relationships with local bookstore owners well ahead of your launch. Talk with local writer friends about which bookstores best support indie authors.

Be creative: Consider other venues as well. For example, if much of your book takes place in a restaurant, ask local restaurants if they would host. A local active senior community might be happy to host an event about your late-life love story. A local library might have a meeting room you can use without cost. Good Vibrations, a women-owned sex toy shop in California, hosted a launch party for *Aphrodite's Pen*, my book about writing seasoned erotica. Many authors host launch parties in their back yards. During the pandemic, online book launches sponsored by bookstores became popular. These days many book launches are hybrid (in person and online).

However you celebrate the launch of your book, have someone take photos or videos of you reading your novel, and use clips to publicize your book on your platform. Use a device that hooks to your phone and allows you to sell your novel from any location. Plan in advance a few fun phrases to write when you sign books. And ask folks who buy your book at an event to review it after they read it.

EXERCISE: PUBLICITY PLANNING

Answer these questions as you continue to prepare to write your marketing plan.

1. Would you prefer to do a launch event as a solo reading, or another format such as an "In Conversation With" presentation? If the latter, whom do you or your publicist know who would be effective at sharing that event with you? Check the Seasoned Romance groups on Facebook for authors of new romance novels.

2. What venues make sense for launch events? Possibly a local bookstore if you have an existing relationship. What bookstores in your area are known to be friendly to local authors? What other organizations connect with your particular book (e.g., if your Well-Seasoned Romance involves aviation history, what museums or other organizations might be interested)? Reach out well in advance of launch.

3. Consider your strengths. How comfortable are you writing

guest blogs? Appearing on podcasts and videocasts? Reaching out to local media, including the event planner at your local bookstore? Doing events such as book readings? Would it help to participate in Toastmasters in advance of publication?

CHAPTER 23
MARKET YOUR WELL-SEASONED ROMANCE

Whether you self-publish or traditionally publish, you will be responsible, in whole or in part, for selling your book. Plan on marketing your book yourself unless you have deep pockets—or your publisher does. Assuming that you want your book read as broadly as possible, and that you want to make some money, the process is a marathon not a sprint.

Spending money to market your books opens up an array of possibilities, not just advertising. Choose judiciously; some of the lower cost methods can be quite effective. Check out the possibilities below to set your marketing priorities in line with your budget. Of course, a traditional publisher should have a budget for paid marketing, but even where this is the case, you will probably need to complement your publisher's efforts with some of your own. This may include advertisements on Amazon, Facebook, and in trade publications.

The definition of Marketing also encompasses strategy: pricing your book, distributing your book, and adjusting your marketing and publicity plan as you track which actions correlate with increased sales.

Taking Stock: Your Personal Inventory

Your first best asset in selling your books is you. And to learn more about yourself as a marketer, take time to ask yourself some questions. What do you want from writing and publishing your Well-Seasoned Romance? What are your strengths as a marketer? Your answers will inform your actions: the audiences you identify, the book descriptions you provide, the keywords you choose, the press releases you send. Your answers are the foundation of your marketing, whether you're marketing to agents and publishers or to readers.

Marketing Begins with Audience

Who reads Seasoned Romance? And who will read your book? How will your target audience know that your book exists?

The number of books being published has climbed massively in the last ten years, in large part because of self-publishing. At the same time, the average American is reading fewer books (although Romance readers continue to read far more books than average). So it's extra important to think strategically about your audience, and to aim your marketing where your readers are. Here are questions to consider.

- **Where does your target audience go for information and entertainment?** This could include free publicity resources (such as Facebook groups) as well as paid venues (such as targeted ads on Facebook, BookBub, Amazon, etc.). *Smart Bitches Trashy Books*, a website for Romance readers that has been featured in *USA Today*, *The New Yorker*, *The New York Times*, *The Washington Post*, *Metro:New York*, *Salon*, and in forums dedicated to "the finest online wankage money can't buy," gets over 350,000 views a month, and an ad costs $75. No demographic breakdown is available, but still, $75. As with all advertising, make sure you track the results of your spend — even a modest spend.

- **Who are the influencers for your target market, and how will you cultivate them?** Follow authors like Freya Sampson (*The Lost Ticket*), Roselle Lim (*Sophie Go's Lonely Hearts Club*), and Beth O'Leary (*The Switch*). You can share their posts, buy and review their books, and contact them directly with useful information.

Your Fan Club

Some of your readers will also become your fans—people who are ready to be Beta readers, and who will not only buy but also review and share about your books. These folks will gladly join your email list if you ask, via social media and by those annoying pop-ups you can set up on your website. These enthusiastic followers are one reason your mailing list is such a valuable asset. You can use a paid service such as MailerLite (my preferred service) or MailChimp to distribute content to your mailing list (there are many others; check them out and find your best fit). From there, you can ask for book sales and reviews as part of each monthly newsletter.

Branding

An author is a brand. Everything you do or say online affects your brand. So brand in a way that connects with your audience.

- Whether or not you write under a pen name, your brand is your author's personality—not necessarily your own.
- Your brand needs to be consistent across all platforms, though you can emphasize different aspects of personality to match the platform you are using (For example, you can be a bit more snarky on Instagram, whereas LinkedIn is more staid).
- Building a brand includes building relationships. Every interaction affects your brand. How you interact with booksellers, with other authors, and with your followers

should reflect both your author voice and your gratitude for their support.

Your brand will change over time. Mine has evolved from Elderotica author to Romance author, with a strong through-line of advocacy for older women.

Book Metadata

Metadata is the way search engines recommend your book to readers. It includes everything from your title, your ISBN number, and your book description, all the way to your author bio. Managing metadata is a strategic marketing function.

Two parts of your metadata that need particular focus are your keywords and your book categories.

- **Keywords** are the words you expect your readers will use to search for books like yours. For ideas, you can look at words used in the descriptions of Seasoned Romance novels that are thematically close to yours. You will want to use keywords in your book description, your author bio, and your publicity materials. You will also input keywords when you upload your book into online stores such as Amazon. Keywords can pertain to setting (e.g., medieval England), characters (vampire, scientist), character roles (strong female lead, Lesbian), plot themes (age playfully), and the tone of the story (rebellious, feminist). To maximize the amount of searchable information about your book, avoid repeating words used in your categories.
- **Categories** are specific to each online publisher and are the particular niches within genres into which your book fits. You can look up the full list of categories for each online store where you plan to sell your book. Keep in mind that these change from time to time. For example, currently some of the categories that may be useful for Amazon are

Later in Life Romance, Second Chance Romance, and Starting Over Romance. Amazon stacks terms in a hierarchy to create more specific categories where there are fewer books and less competition. One category for *Vampires of a Certain Age*, for example, could be Paranormal Vampire Romance. Another could be Later in Life Paranormal Romance. Amazon allows you to list your book by two categories automatically, and you can (and should) call their Customer Service to request an additional eight categories. The ideal category would have lots of readers and few competitors. Categories vary between online sellers (Barnes & Noble, AppleBooks, Kobo, etc.), so have some alternatives planned.

Pricing

How much your book costs will affect how many copies you sell. For e-books, there is a sweet spot for pricing which is around where your comps are selling. If your price is way higher or way lower, you may discourage your target audience.

Also keep in mind the e-book price structure built into online store incentives. For example, as of this writing, the royalty percentage for Amazon (the gorilla in the room) is higher for e-books priced between $2.99 and $9.99.

For paperbacks, pricing is complicated by the costs involved, including the rising cost of paper, which is factored into the amount each POD copy costs to produce. Even traditional publishers look askance at books over 80,000 words these days because of paper costs. You can, of course, restrict your publishing to the e-book format. But if you publish your novel as a paperback too, make sure you price it so that you make at least some profit.

Distribution

Distribution is a key part of your marketing strategy and will look different depending on the publication route. With a traditional publisher, distribution will be more focused on bookstores, whereas an indie published book is more focused on online sales.

Given the dominance of Amazon in the online marketplace, if you are an indie author, a key decision is whether or not to distribute exclusively with Amazon through their KDP Select program. If you sign a 90-day contract with KDP Select, your e-book can only be sold on Amazon during that time. In addition, it will be available to Kindle Unlimited readers, who pay a fixed amount (currently $11.99 a month) for unlimited access to all books in the program. Authors who have used KDP Select say that it is easy to use, and you will have access to a number of Kindle Unlimited readers on fixed incomes who read voraciously but only on KU. On the other hand, if you start your novel on KDP Select, you lose the opportunity to build a following on platforms like Barnes & Noble and Kobo. Plus, if you decide to go wide later, you may have a hard time convincing your followers to pay for your books when they have been reading them for "free."

If you go wide and publish in multiple online stores, you will need to decide whether to use an aggregator, a company that will distribute your book to multiple online stores. Using an aggregator simplifies the process but will consume a percentage of your revenues. For more about aggregators, please refer back to Chapter Nineteen.

More and more authors are distributing via their own websites. One obvious advantage is that you make more money on each sale than selling via an online store. In addition, selling direct means you know who bought your book. You have their email address and can encourage them to join your mailing list. You can thank them for their purchase and ask them to review your book. You can let them know when the next in your series launches. And of course, you can continue to distribute widely through other online stores while you offer your books on your own website. If you decide to add direct sales to your distribution channels, there are several companies set up to assist.

Book Giveaway

Hosting a giveaway of your new novel can generate excitement about your book, and depending on how you structure it, can also lead to new names on your mailing list and a boost in sales. It's also a great way to thank your readers for their support. Decide on a platform for your giveaway, such as Goodreads or BookFunnel. Then design the graphics to announce the giveaway. Canva has a selection of book giveaway templates you can customize. Use your graphics to publicize your giveaway, including the rules (e.g., you'll be added to the mailing list if you enter), and how many e-books you are giving away. Reach out to other authors to ask if they are willing to share out your giveaway (Be sure to offer to publicize their giveaways as well). Over the course of the campaign, keep up the excitement by updating your social media platform with how many copies remain to be given away.

And at the end, don't just send out the books. Write to everyone who entered and thank them—and offer those who did not win a discount coupon for your book.

Advertising

Only you can determine what advertising budget is comfortable for your first book. Once you have established that, you can use paid advertising to create buzz before your launch. Target your audience by demographics on FaceBook, BookBub and Amazon.

Be sure to measure and track the effectiveness of your advertisements. Correlate your book sales with your advertisements to determine which ads (and which venues) are most effective. Draft2Digital (a POD printer that distributes print and ebooks) currently provides daily sales breakdowns, which makes it easy to check advertising effectiveness. Once you have that information, do more of what works. If something isn't working, tweak the advertising image and/or wording and see if that improves results. After you've tried the tweaks, stop the advertisements that do not perform.

Allied with advertising is the **paid review**. You can use a paid service for reviews, such as Book Siren. You can pay Book Siren to distribute e-books to readers who will review your book on online stores.

Another approach is a **book trailer**, a brief video you produce. Watch other book trailers to see what you like, and think about how to present your book. You can spring for software that makes it easier to create a book trailer. You can incorporate video of yourself talking about your book and reading from your book. And you can include free music and photos from Pixabay. If you have taken your own photographs of the setting of your book, those can also be incorporated into your video.

Use a Scheduling Program for Consistent, Sustained Content

For both marketing and publicity, consistent appearances on your platform are important to keep your author brand fresh with your readers. I share a meme and repost a relevant article on social media every day—which does not mean I spend time on each site every day. There are several programs you can buy that enable you to schedule posts ahead of time, with flexibility to change the schedule as needed (I use PostPlanner). I also send blogs to my mailing list on the tenth and twentieth of each month and a newsletter on the thirtieth, so my mailing list hears from me every ten days. As those blogs and newsletters publish, I set them up to distribute on FaceBook, LinkedIn and X through PostPlanner. And while a tool like PostPlanner is great to ensure consistent posting, it is also important to interact regularly with supporters who comment on your posts.

In addition to your social media platform, you can share content about your new novel to author pages on these sites:

- Amazon.
- Barnes & Noble.
- Goodreads (Goodreads can be set up to feed your blog onto their site).
- Rakuten Kobo.

Keep Writing Books

The best thing you can do to market your book is to write another, and another after that. Series do especially well in the Romance genre because Romance readers read so many books. Are there other stories to tell about your sidekicks, or about other minor characters in your story? In the case of *Vampires of a Certain Age*, the vampire sisterhood from medieval Yorkshire is a rich source for new stories.

So keep the pen moving, or the keys clicking! You have more tales of Seasoned Romance to tell.

Marketing Planning

Now that you have reviewed many ways to publicize and market your book, you are ready to create a marketing plan and timeline. As you generate and implement this plan, coordinate with your traditional publisher or your publicist about marketing strategy and execution. But keep in mind that your traditional publisher will hang in for about three months before they move on to the next book—and you will want to keep your marketing train going.

Even some traditionally published authors hire a publicist to increase their visibility. Anybody can all themselves a publicist, but the best of the bunch have top reviewers on Speed Dial and connections with big book clubs like Oprah's. Book a year in advance and expect to spend $5K to $20K.

Keep in mind that even the best marketing plan needs adjusting. Measure and track results and modify your plan accordingly. Try things. What's the outcome? For example, LinkedIn gives you a weekly readout of which posts achieved the most engagement. You can share other's articles and add your own caption to connect with your own related blog or book. Tweak what you're doing; if it still doesn't work, focus somewhere else. *Measure results not activity.*

AUTHOR'S CRAFT: CREATE A PUBLICITY AND MARKETING PLAN

After reviewing the chapters on publicity and marketing, use the list below to develop a marketing plan for your launch. If you have a publicist, review a draft with them and coordinate tasks. As you execute your plan, revisit it often to refine it based on tracking results, and be open to trying new ways to reach your audience and to developing new skills.

More Than Six Months Before Launch (as soon as you decide to write a book):

- Build author website and begin writing blogs.
- Build network of contacts with influencers, target audience, potential reviewers.
- Build email list based on your blog.

Six Months Pre-Launch:

- Update author website and blog.
- Prepare Publicity Materials, Book Pages, Author Pages, Press Kit.

Four Months Pre-Launch:

- Cover reveal.
- Share Advance Review Copies (ARCs) and Press Kit with reviewers, influencers.
- Invite endorsements from other authors, influencers.
- Share ARCs and Press Kit with podcasters and ask to be invited near launch.

- Plan book launch events.

Three Months Pre-Launch:

- Start countdown on your social media platforms and in your newsletter.
- Share visuals with early review clips on social media.
- Write guest blogs that include launch announcement.

Two Months Pre-Launch:

- Ask influencers and others in your network to get the word out.
- Announce guest appearances in advance.
- Post your Press Kit on your web site and share it with media outlets.

One Month Pre-Launch:

- Begin guest blogs and appearances.
- Announce launch events in your newsletter and on social media.
- Set up Pre-sales of your book on Amazon to boost launch sales figures.
- Share book trailer and reels on social media, and add to your website.

At Launch:

- Launch Events.
- Book sales/discounts.

- Social media promotion.
- Paid advertising.
- Book giveaway on Goodreads or BookFunnel.

Post-Launch:

- Continue to showcase your book through podcasts, on your website.
- Add visuals with additional positive clips from new reviews to Instagram, etc.
- Keep your website up to date with links to new appearances.

A Final Note on Marketing Strategy: Create a way to track your publicity and marketing efforts. Set up a spreadsheet with pages such as Reviewers, Podcasts, Book Groups, Paid Advertising, etc. Depending on the page, record different data points in the columns. For Podcasts, for example, record the host name and contact information, the date you emailed them, the response and date, the date an e-book was sent, the date of each appearance, and the link to the appearance, the date shared to social media and your newsletter.

PART FOUR: CONCLUSION & RESOURCES

The marketing journey for your Well-Seasoned Romance involves many decisions about pricing, distribution channels, and outreach via free publicity and paid advertising. Many of these choices will be open to change. Experiment and learn as you go.

But the basics will always be there: networking, consistent connection with your readers, and showing your gratitude to the folks who support you on your journey. And always remember that the best marketing is your next book. Onward!

Part Four Resources

Magazines and podcasts come and go; be sure to supplement this list with your own findings.

Podcasts that Focus on Women Past Midlife (Including Authors)

- Badass Women at Any Age — Bonnie Marcus (https://podcasts.apple.com/us/podcast/badass-women-at-any-age/id1480376047).
- Yvonne Marchese on her Late Bloomer Living podcast (https://www.latebloomerliving.com/podcast/).

- Zestful Aging with Nicole Christina (https://zestfulaging.com/podcast/).
- Hey Boomer with Wendy Green (https://heyboomer.biz).
- Off Air with Jan and Fi (https://www.thetimes.co.uk/podcasts/off-air-with-jane-and-fi).
- Twisting the Plot (https://twistingtheplot.com/podcasts/).
- Why Didn't Anyone Tell Me This? (https://joyceharper.com/podcasts/).
- Hot Flashes and Cool Topics (https://hotflashescooltopics.com).
- Your Next Chapter (https://www.angelaraspass.com.au/podcasts/).
- Women Over 70 Podcast (https://womenover70.com).
- Midlife Confidential (interview show from CrunchyTales Magazine) (https://www.youtube.com/watch?v=5TSg0A8TmBU&list=PLZd69Fb37HE6hVzNS0Y0CF6WEV4gydzjP&index=3).
- Diana Wilde — Granny's Got a Podcast (https://podcasters.spotify.com/pod/show/diana-wilde9).
- Elizabeth Holmes Radiant Badass (https://radiantbadass.com/podcast/).
- Nancy Shenker — The Geezer Proofer (https://podcasts.apple.com/us/podcast/the-geezer-proofer/id1706589864).
- Older Women and Friends with Jane Leder (https://www.olderwomenandfriends.net).
- Glorious Broads — Maryjane Fahey (https://www.gloriousbroads.com).

Podcasts about Romance Novels

- Smart Podcast, Trashy Books (https://smartbitchestrashybooks.com/podcast/).
- Book Thingo Podcast (https://bookthingo.com.au/podcasts/).

- Not Now, I'm Reading (https://nnirpodcast.wordpress.com).
- Smart Women Read Romance (https://podcasts.apple.com/us/podcast/smart-women-read-romance/id1447111587).
- When in Romance (https://podcasts.apple.com/us/podcast/when-in-romance/id1338807540).

Online Magazines that Feature Women Past Midlife

- CrunchyTales Magazine: (https://www.crunchytales.com).
- Certain Age Magazine: (https://www.certainagemag.com).
- The Pro-Age Woman: (https://theproagewoman.com).

Creative Resources

Canva - for creation of memes for social media: (www.canva.com).

Pixabay - source of royalty-free photographs and music: (https://pixabay.com).

GLOSSARY OF TERMS AND ABBREVIATIONS

Act One: In Romance, introduces each main character to the reader, then shows their meeting under circumstances that introduce conflict.

Act Two: In Romance, provides a series of conflicts and resolutions based primarily on the internal plot and secondarily upon the external plot.

Act Three: In Romance, the "Happy For Now" or "Happily Ever After" ending; may conclude with an Epilogue showing the couple's happy future.

Advance: The amount a traditional publisher pays to an author before publication. Typically based on expectations for first year sales, and typically paid by a medium to large publishing house.

Advance Review Copy (ARC): Pre-publication version of an upcoming book sent to reviewers before the final proofread. Can be an e-book or a physical copy. Should be clearly marked on the front cover as a review copy, not for sale.

GLOSSARY OF TERMS AND ABBREVIATIONS

Agent: See **Literary Agent**.

Antagonist: The character who is a source of conflict in a novel. In Romance, both main characters are antagonists (and **Protagonists**).

Author Bio: Roughly two paragraph biography of the author, written in third person, that highlights their accomplishments and ends with ways to connect on the author's platform.

Author Page: The location on an online store or book-related website (e.g., Goodreads) that displays information about the author.

Author Platform: Author's presence including publications, social media, relationships with other authors, and the author's ability to influence others (for example, via blogging and through podcast appearances).

Autofiction: Fiction loosely based on conflicts, individuals and places in the author's own history, often constructed in a mix-and-match fashion. The word "autofiction" combines autobiography and fiction.

Back Matter: The pages in a book that appear after the main text. May include Acknowledgements, About the Author, Discussion Questions, etc. See also **Front Matter**.

Backstory: The history of a character, often developed by an author before writing a book. The author may strategically share parts of the backstory in the text of the book.

Beta Reader: A person who reads a manuscript when it is nearing completion and provides suggestions to the author, usually without compensation.

Book Description (Elevator Pitch): A quick, punchy set of statements designed to sell a book. It is engaging and provides all relevant information, but does not reveal the ending of the book. Used in publicity and on the back cover. See also **Synopsis**.

Book Page: The location on an online store or book-related website (e.g., Goodreads) that displays information about a book.

Book Review: A written reaction to a book, either by a professional reviewer or posted by a reader on an online store or book-related website (e.g., Goodreads).

Brief: A set of instructions an author provides to a creative contractor (e.g., a book cover designer).

Blurb (or **Endorsement**)**:** A few sentences by a reviewer or by another author promoting a book, to be used in publicity.

Character Arc: The storyline for a particular character, as distinct from the overall plot of the story.

Characters A and B: In Romance, the main characters who will experience conflicts and resolutions with one another, leading ultimately to the happy ending. In Romance, these two characters are both the **Protagonists** and the **Antagonists**.

Counter Trope: Term for a premise that is the opposite of what is expected in a genre. One example for Well-Seasoned Romance: A woman over sixty must choose between several possible lovers.

Developmental Editing: The first stage of editing in which the contents may be expanded to include overlooked story elements and contracted to eliminate extraneous matter. The sequence of the story may also be changed and optimized. See also **Line Editing** and **Proofreading**.

GLOSSARY OF TERMS AND ABBREVIATIONS

Elevator Pitch (Book Description): A quick, punchy set of statements designed to sell a book. It is engaging and provides all relevant information, but does not reveal the ending of the book. Used in publicity and on the back cover. See also **Synopsis**.

Endorsement (or **Blurb**): A few sentences by a reviewer or by another author promoting a book, to be used in publicity.

Epilogue: An optional sequence at the end of **Act Three** of a Romance that shows the continued happiness of the main characters after the denouement.

External Conflict: In Romance, a secondary source of friction beyond the internal conflict experienced by the main characters.

External Plot: A plot built on circumstances outside the conflict between the main characters. In Romance, the external plot is secondary and the plot based on conflict between the main characters is the primary driver.

Fair Use: Quotation in a book of a limited amount of text from another author, that is not yet in the public domain. Fair Use is often litigated and authors should take advice from legal counsel before using quotations without permission from the copyright holder.

Front Matter: The pages in a book that appear before the main text. May include the Title Page, a list of other books by the author, a Dedication, the Table of Contents, etc. See also **Back Matter**.

Happily Ever After Ending (HEA): The traditional conclusion of a Romance novel, complete with wedding.

Happy For Now Ending (HFN): A more modern ending to a Romance. The main characters are joyfully romantically involved at the end of the story. While indications are that the relationship will be successful, the main characters do not marry during the story.

Hybrid Publishing: This publication model is midway on a continuum between indie and traditional publishing. Hybrid publishers are selective and provide services to authors for payment. Royalties are higher than for a **Traditional Publisher**. See also the standards discussed under **IBPA**.

Independent Book Publishers Association (IBPA): An organization that represents the interests of indie or self published authors. The IBPA website includes a list of criteria that differentiates a hybrid publisher from a **Vanity Press.**

Indie Publishing (Self-Publishing): In this publishing model, the author is in charge of all aspects from writing to editing to publishing to marketing. The author may choose to hire contractors (such as an editor or a cover designer) for certain aspects of creating and selling the book.

Inner Conflict: The conflict each of the main characters experiences regarding the relationship, which may be based on each character's backstory.

Inner Critic: A perfectionistic personality aspect which is best engaged at the proofreading stage of creating a book.

Inner Wound: A challenge in a character's **Backstory** that contributes to conflict in the Romance plot.

Internal Conflict: The conflict which arises between the main characters, based on their **Backstory** and/or their current roles.

Internal Plot: The storyline based on the back-and-forth between the main characters. Each character's ambivalence is based at least in part

GLOSSARY OF TERMS AND ABBREVIATIONS

on their history (**Backstory**). In Romance, the internal plot is primary and the **External Plot** is secondary. At least one perceived betrayal is typically part of the internal plot of a Romance.

International Standard Book Number (ISBN): A product identifier used by bookstores and online stores to order books. In the United States, publishers and indie authors typically purchase ISBNs from Bowker, the official source for the US.

Keywords: Words or phrases that readers are likely to use when searching online for a certain type of book. Determining the best keywords for a book is part of the marketing effort.

Later in Life Romance: Another term for **Seasoned Romance**.

Line Editing: In the second phase of editing, the focus is on optimizing each line of text. See also **Developmental Editing** and **Proofreading**.

Literary Agent: An agent evaluates books submitted by authors. If an agent decides to take on a client and their book, the agent will likely suggest edits before submitting the book to publishers. Top agents have access to publishers who do not accept manuscripts directly from writers. Agents are compensated through an agreed upon percentage of the **Advance** and **Royalties**.

Logline: The novel's concept boiled down to one or two sentences. See also **Tagline** and **Elevator Pitch**.

Marketing: Includes both paid advertising and strategizing (such as optimizing **Keywords** and tracking the effectiveness of different promotions).

Meet Cute: A memorable first encounter between the main characters in Act One of a Romance novel, often with awkward or humorous overtones. In a Well-Seasoned Romance, however, in which the main characters have already led full lives, "When Worlds Collide" may be a better term.

Meme: An image that may include text, a graphic, and/or a photo, that may spread rapidly online. Authors or publicists may create memes as part of the publicity for a book via an online site such as Canva.com.

Metadata: Data that describes a book, such as the title, the name of the author, the **ISBN**, the price, the genre, etc.

National Novel Writing Month (NaNoWriMo): A free online event in which writers pledge to write 50,000 words during November. NaNoWriMo provides free resources for writers.

Premise: A sentence that captures the main idea for a story.

Print on Demand (POD): An alternative to the traditional print run in which each copy of a book is created and shipped after it is ordered.

Press Kit: Materials sent to media outlets to announce a book launch. May include a press release, the offer of an **Advance Review Copy** (ebook or print), a page with the title of the book and its Table of Contents, (if any), a brief excerpt from the novel, and a page of suggested interview questions.

Press Release: Used to announce the launch of a novel, a Press Release typically includes the launch date, a thumbnail view of the front cover, the available formats (paperback, e-book, audio, etc.), the **ISBN** and price for each format, where distributed, the number of pages, the genre and sub-genre, the **Logline**, **Tagline**, and **Elevator Pitch**, advance praise about the book, and information about the author including a headshot, social media presence and contact information.

Proofreading: The last of three phases of editing. Proofreading focuses on correct syntax, grammar, spelling, and punctuation. See also **Developmental Editing** and **Line Editing**.

Protagonist: The character who resolves conflicts in a novel. In Romance, both main characters are protagonists (and **Antagonists**).

Public Domain: Books and other creative materials enter the public domain when their copyright expires, or when their author explicitly places the work in the public domain. This material is eligible for quotation with attribution but without obtaining permission from the author.

Publicity: Unpaid promotion of a book, including free use of social media, outreach to the author's mailing list, blogs and guest blogs, as well as appearances on podcasts and other interviews. Also includes unpaid reviews of a book.

Query Letter: The letter a writer sends to a **Literary Agent** or publisher requesting them to consider publishing a book. The letter should show the writer's command of language, explain how the book is suited to this agent or publisher, and demonstrate that the book is interesting and worth their time to consider.

Reel: A very short video; can be used on social media to promote a book.

Reversion of Rights: A provision in a publishing contract that details the circumstances under which the right to publish a book reverts from the publisher to the author.

Rights (Primary, Subsidiary, Territorial): The exclusive ability to publish a book in certain formats or places. The first draft contract a writer receives from a publisher may ask for rights to all formats in all markets around the world. Negotiation of these rights is a key part of a literary agent's or attorney's role in representing an author.

Romance Novel: A book that follows a predetermined structure, where the main plot driver is the relationship between the main characters, and which ultimately arrives at a happy ending (**HEA** or **HFN**). See also **Act One**, **Act Two**, and **Act Three**.

Romance Trope: The essential plot concept for a Romance novel. Examples that are useful in **Well-Seasoned Romance** include Enemies-to-Lovers, Friends-to-Lovers, and Second Chance Romance.

Romantic Tension: The gradual buildup of libido through the twists and turns in a Romance plot.

Royalty: Percentage of book revenues paid to an author by a traditional or hybrid publisher.

Seasoned Romance: In publishing, a Seasoned Romance features main characters in their thirties, forties, or older. See also **Well-Seasoned Romance**.

Second Chance Romance: A Romance story in which two characters who met in their youth and lost track of one another reconnect later in life.

Self-Publishing: See **Indie Publishing.**

Sidekick Character: The confidante of a main character. The author may use a sidekick to introduce backstory about a main character. A sidekick may also be involved in a secondary romance.

GLOSSARY OF TERMS AND ABBREVIATIONS

Synopsis: A book description that includes the denouement of the story. This is used to pitch a book to an agent or publisher, and does not appear in marketing to potential readers. By contrast, see **Elevator Pitch (Book Description)** for material used in general marketing.

Three Act Structure: The beginning (**Act One**), middle (**Act Two**) and end (**Act Three**) of a story.

Tagline: A short, clever line about a book, used in marketing and publicity. The tagline is meant to engage interest and only hints at the content of the story. See also **Logline** and **Elevator Pitch**.

Traditional Publisher: A publishing house that fronts the cost of editing, production, marketing and publicity of a book in exchange for a high percentage of revenues. Some traditional publishers pay an **Advance** to authors as well as **Royalties** (after the book has earned its advance).

Vanity Press: A hired printer that does not meet the **IBPA** standards for a hybrid publisher.

Warranties and Indemnifications: Representations made by an author in a publishing contract, and which should be vetted by a literary attorney as part of a full contract review.

Well-Seasoned Romance: As used in this book, a Well-Seasoned Romance features main characters in their fifties, sixties, or older.

ABOUT THE AUTHOR

Stella Fosse

Stella Fosse is the *nom de plume* of an author of a certain age, who in her sixties started writing sexy stories as a creative antidote to the ageism and sexism older women face in society. She champions older women's creativity by leading workshops in seasoned romance, erotica, and memoir writing.

Stella is a frequent guest on podcasts for women past midlife. She has been published in many online venues. Stella also blogs about issues of interest to Women of a Certain Age, including creativity, romance, and older women's health.

Her new book *Write & Sell a Well-Seasoned Romance* empowers women to tell vivid stories of late life love.

Traditionally published works include her book *Aphrodite's Pen: The Power of Writing Erotica after Midlife*. Stella's story collection, *The*

Erotic Pandemic Collection, is an imaginative exploration of romance in quarantine. Her first novel, *Brilliant Charming Bastard*, is a nerdy, romantic escapade through the San Francisco biotech scene. Her second novel, *Vampires of a Certain Age*, expands her exploration of the vivid lives of older women.

Stella hails from California and shares the joy and empowerment of writing past midlife with women in her adopted state of North Carolina. She enjoys gathering online with women all over the world to write and laugh together.

Stella's books are available at your local bookseller and your favorite online place. She shares her writing, as well as ideas and resources for empowering women past midlife, at www.stellafosse.com.

Please join Stella on social media here:

- facebook.com/StellaFosseAuthor
- instagram.com/stella.fosse
- goodreads.com/stellafosse
- linkedin.com/in/StellaFosse
- amazon.com/stores/Stella-Fosse/author/B07NKSTDQC
- bookbub.com/authors/stella-fosse
- x.com/stellafosse

STELLA WOULD LOVE TO KNOW YOU BETTER!

Stella writes a regular blog and newsletter. A blog comes out—either from her or from a guest blogger[1]—on the 10th and 20th of the month. That's always related to being a woman past mid-life or the craft of writing [you can find Stella's manifesto here:

[https://stellafosse.com/stella-fosse-author-erotic-writer/#Manifesto].

Stella's newsletter publishes at the end of each month.

You can sign up for Stella's newsletter & blog here:

[https://page.stellafosse.com/ebook].

---

1. Want to write a guest blog? Stella welcomes drafts or suggestions for promoting your writing or thoughts there. You should be 'on topic' for her blog - see her manifesto [https://stellafosse.com/stella-fosse-author-erotic-writer/#Manifesto] for the topics that she covers on her blog and website. The requirements for submission are here [https://stellafosse.com/stella-fosse-author/#Submissions].

PLEASE REVIEW THIS BOOK

A Review is one of the biggest favors you can do for an author—especially on the larger vendors' sites.

Reviews are the lifeblood of writers because they let other readers—and potential readers—know what you thought of their work. Some topics to consider:

What struck you about this book?

How useful is the information on creating a Well-Seasoned Romance?

What was your opinion of the writing?

How about the editing?

What do you want to say about this book to other readers?

Please write an honest review on whichever web platform you prefer. Stella is on all the major platforms and you know *your* favorites! Stella is also on Goodreads [https://www.goodreads.com/stellafosse] & BookBub [https://www.bookbub.com/authors/stella-fosse].

ACKNOWLEDGMENTS

The best thing about writing a book about writing is sharing the manuscript with other writers. The writers who thank you for giving them new ideas spur you on to greater things. And the writers who give you more ideas are worth their weight in gold. All the writers and authors in these acknowledgments were generous with their time and gifts.

I am blessed with a terrific critique group here in North Carolina. These women waded through various chapter versions with enthusiasm and great suggestions. Mirinda Kossoff, Donna Miller, Dona Carol and Julia Hardie have ably seen me through several incarnations of this work. Several of them even double-dipped and commented on the Beta version when it was ready.

Speaking of which, we had a fantastic group of Beta readers who provided so many valuable comments. Huge thanks to all these folks for their skilled reviews: Barb Papajohn Gerron, Gary Wedlund, Nivedita Mishra, Karen Smiley, Donna Childs, and Patricia Grayhall each added much value to the final manuscript. And particular kudos to Samantha Dunaway Bryant, who may be the first to start writing a Well-Seasoned Romance with guidance from this book, before it was even published!

My friend Judith Stanton, editor extraordinaire, made great content and line edit suggestions. Judith is both an author (*A Stallion to Die*

For) and a former English professor, and no typo escapes her eagle eye.

And, as always, thank to my friends from the Dirty Old Women reading series, who later became the Elderotica writers. Lynx Canon, Charli Allan, Billie Berlin, Dorothy Freed, Rene Johns, Sue Kay, Rose Mark, Fran Spector, Chris Orr, Jan Steckel and Mya Thomae have been my guiding lights throughout both my books on writing: this volume and its predecessor, *Aphrodite's Pen: The Power of Writing Erotica after Midlife*.

And finally, huge thanks to my best friend, my partner in life and in publishing, the inimitable Graham Bird. No writer ever had such support in this independent publishing adventure.

Writing, editing, publishing and marketing *Write & Sell a Well-Seasoned Romance* has been and will be a grand escapade. A heart-felt thank you to everyone who helped make this book a reality. May this book in turn help launch many grand tales of late life love.

www.ingramcontent.com/pod-product-compliance
Lightning Source LLC
Chambersburg PA
CBHW070050080526
44586CB00013B/1000